A Thesaurus of Women

from Water to Music

A Thesaurus of Women

from Water to Music

Barbara Joan Zeitz, M.A.

A Thesaurus of Women
From Water to Music

iUniverse books may be ordered through booksellers or by contacting:

iUniverse
1663 Liberty Drive
Bloomington, IN 47403
www.iuniverse.com
1-800-Authors (1-800-288-4677)

ISBN: 978-1-4917-9642-9 (sc)
ISBN: 978-1-4917-9641-2 (e)

Library of Congress Control Number: 2016909788

Print information available on the last page.

iUniverse rev. date: 09/08/2016

Dedicated to
and in
appreciation of
all the women never encouraged or supported
to contribute,
then never acknowledged
for their countless contributions.

Contents

Preface

~

When I published my first book in 2012, *A Thesaurus of Women from Cherry Blossoms to Cell Phones*, an anthology of my monthly online "CountHerhistory" column I began in 2003, it was intended to serve as my legacy of the women's history work that had come to define the final career of my life; that of researching, writing and, most importantly, sharing the hidden history of women and their overlooked accomplishments, that had been all but left out of traditional history books.

But as my monthly online columns grew in number, a second book clambered to be part of my legacy. So many more women needed to be properly acknowledged in a book. For me to ignore them and their accomplishments would be as odious as their original omission from traditional history books. Moreover, it would be an affront to the women's history I was writing to "right" that wrongful omission. Thus, began my endeavors to produce and self-publish this, my second book *A Thesaurus of Women from Water to Music*.

Water to Music, just like *Cherry Blossoms to Cell Phones*, is a collection of fifty-two "CountHerhistory" columns, basically the second fifty-two. That number, as before, was chosen based on the number of weeks in a year and to be respectful of the women whose busy, multitasking schedules allow for little time to curl up with a good book.

Either of my good books can be read in one curled-up reading, of course (and it has been done), but they can also be picked up and put down repeatedly, perhaps fifty-two times, without interruption to story continuity. Each chapter is written in an easy-to-read, mini-novella style with a beginning, middle, and end. Either book offers a morning, an afternoon, an evening, or a full year of women's history one week at a time. And while each chapter stands alone, a ribbon of gender runs through them all.

For the most part, the chapters appear in the order in which they were written as columns. However, certain chapters were repositioned to coincide with dates such as Mother's Day, D-Day, Black History Month, and the like. The first and last chapters were chosen to correspond to the title, just as in my first book.

As in *Cherry Blossoms to Cell Phones*, the topics were chosen based on a variety of reasons. Many stemmed from my own curiosity. When I would hear the name of a woman I did not recognize, only to learn through research that hers was a name I should have known, thus a woman you should know, a column was born. For example, when I learned the woman about to become America's First Lady was a descendant of America's institution of plantation slavery, I took a closer look at the history of America's first First Lady and the plantation slaves she owned.

And while in *Cherry Blossoms to Cell Phones*, I had written about some of the many important historic accomplishments of black women, in *Water to Music*, I delved deeper into their history and also expanded my research with a special emphasis on diversity, seeking out women from multiple cultures. This research produced columns recognizing women of Asian and Middle Eastern cultures and more equally represented Native American Indian, Black, and Hispanic women's historic accomplishments.

During the heavy media coverage of the Arab Spring and a focus on veiled women in modern-day and Ancient Egypt, I went back in time and found that, long before 2011, veiled Egyptian women protested in the streets and removed the veil. That surprised me, and I suspected it would surprise you also.

Other topics were developed when I considered the celebration of special days, such as D-day, with little reference to women. I would ask myself, were any women and their contributions to that day worthy of mention? Of course there were, so I mentioned them. At the 150th commemoration of the Medal of Honor, the highest military honor in the United States, awarded for acts of valor above and beyond the call of duty, I wondered if any of the 3,475 medals awarded had been awarded to women. I learned that one had, and I felt compelled to tell you of this Civil War female surgeon.

I researched military women in the United States of America and the culture of gender abuse and rejection they fought against in order to serve their country—only to continue to be subjected to an atmosphere of gender abuse as they officially serve. I then looked at women who served, and/or attempted to serve, in elected office and wrote of women who have been elected mayors of major cities and women who have campaigned to be elected president.

When, in 2013, I became aware that only 20 women senators were serving in the United States Senate, I was curious and furious. I decided to research just how many women senators had served in total. I was *appalled* to learn that only 44 women (as compared to 1,902 men) had *ever* been elected to the US Senate. My outrage led to columns on women US senators, representatives, and governors—columns that looked at which states had previously voted women into office and at states still poised to vote women into office in upcoming elections.

Scientific achievements of women—for example, the development of Kevlar, the discovery of the determining genetic sex chromosomal structure, the identification of cloud composition, the explanation of the hot tower power in a hurricane eye, and the pioneering of the first weather satellite—continued to surface. These are recorded in several chapters.

And so my second *Thesaurus of Women*, as did my first, spotlights accomplished, virtually unknown women and links them to well-known aspects of history. And as in *Cherry Blossoms to Cell Phones*, my writings in *Water to Music* are intended to enrich women's lives, simply by giving women their history so that they may take pride in it and, thereby, pride in themselves. I want every woman to know her history and feel the pride celebrated in this, my second book.

I wrote this book for every woman who has stood in awe of the magnificent Hoover Dam not knowing its first draft construction was the work of a woman. I wrote it for every woman who has loaded and unloaded washing machines and dishwashers, unaware that the inventors of these two appliances intended to free women from the unending, burdensome hard labor of washing clothes and dishes during an era when women's days were consumed by these duties were women. I wrote it so that every woman who uses a computer will know that women created software and so that every woman who checks the weather before planning her day will know it was a woman who pioneered the first weather satellite. I want every woman (and man) who has enjoyed chocolate chip cookies and margaritas to know it was a woman who created that cookie and another who mixed that first margarita. Every woman who has been entertained by performances of *Chicago*, *Mary Poppins*, or *The Sound of Music* should know these iconic productions humbly had their genesis in the written words of women long before being released and revered the world over. I want women to know the role that gender played in all of the above, as well as in the many more accomplishments detailed in the pages of this second *Thesaurus of Women*.

As I researched and wrote, I met many women who, without encouragement, support, or acknowledgment of their historic achievements encouraged and supported me as I began to respect, rather than reject, my own meager accomplishments. And this I wish for you also—that you find a woman, or a bevy of women, who will do the same for you as you read of her/your history.

Your history, *A Thesaurus of Women from Water to Music* is my gift to you. Read it, embrace it, and give it (or another copy) away so that another woman may also know the rich history of women and pass that knowledge on!

Thank you.

bjz

countherhistory.wordpress.com

Introduction

〜

Who had her plan to dam the Colorado River creating a reservoir in the Grand Canyon rejected by the US government five years before a man's plan for the Hoover Dam was accepted?

Who founded America's first black-owned woman's bank?

Who unabashedly reported America's black news items as a 1950s' journalist?

Whose 1909 proposal that a nationwide interracial organization be formed to address the unjust treatment of Negroes led to the formation of the NAACP?

Who founded the first printing business in the colonies (1638, Cambridge, Massachusetts)?

Who published America's first African American newspaper, despite criticism from black men?

Who designed and patented the first *working* washing machine invention?

Who designed and patented the dishwasher that later became a Kitchen Aid?

Who invented the circular saw in the early 1800s?

Who developed the Superman strong but lightweight fiber Kevlar?

Who produced the dough batter that created the first chocolate chip cookie?

Who created the first margarita cocktail?

Who established and celebrated the first Mother's Day on May 10, 1908?

Who landed on the beaches at Normandy during World War II allied invasion?

Who identified how the XX/XY chromosomes determine gender?

Who programmed the first empty computer and created software?

Who rode horseback twice as far as Paul Revere to warn the British were coming?

Who identified the heat thermodynamics that occur in the eye of a hurricane?

Who led the data-collecting mission that developed the first weather satellite?

Who was the only woman awarded the US Congressional Medal of Honor?

Who published her songs under the name of her famous brother Felix?

Who composed a symphony, the first by a black woman performed by a major symphony orchestra?

Who led the Cherokee Nation as its first female deputy chief?

Who wrote the book on which the 1968 TV series *The Flying Nun* was based?

Who wrote the play that turned into the iconic 1975 Broadway musical *Chicago*?

Who wrote the book turned into the iconic 1964 *Mary Poppins* Disney movie?

Who wrote a high school play that became the iconic 1965 *Sound of Music* movie?

She did!

These stories and more are contained in *A Thesaurus of Women from Water to Music*, my second book.

Chapter One
Her Dam Water
~

*T*o dam water was her thing. But in the early 1900s, the US government rejected her patent to detour the Colorado River into a reservoir in the Grand Canyon. Harriet Russell Strong had patents for several different types of dams and water storage systems. She was an engineer who believed in water conservation and irrigation by natural water sources. Her innovative irrigation technologies would revamp California's thirsty terrain into irrigated cropland and lay the groundwork for irrefutably the greatest dam in America.

Born in 1844 in Buffalo, New York, Harriet went west to California as an eight-year-old with her family and grew up in mining communities along the California-Nevada border. When she was seventeen, Harriet's family moved to Carson City, Nevada, where she met and, two years later, married Charles Lyman Strong, a man eighteen years her senior.

Charles had made a fortune in banking, publishing, and mining, but mining had taken its toll on his health. He moved Harriet and their first two daughters to the San Gabriel Valley in California, where he and Harriet purchased a 325-acre ranch. She searched for a stable crop to farm and chose walnuts. Walnut plants require constant moisture, for which Harriet designed a suitable irrigation system.

The key to her design was that each dam section was to be structurally supported by the water pressure from the adjoining preceding dam. Her design allowed for a controlled and uniform regulation of water flow and introduced continuous winter irrigation on their ranch.

But Charles soon became bored. He often was away from the ranch for extended periods, as he followed quixotic leads attempting to strike it rich in mining. But instead of fortune, he found debt, a debt he dramatically increased when, without Harriet's knowledge, he borrowed heavily against their ranch to invest in a number of business ventures that failed. He took his life in 1883, leaving Harriet a single mom and a mountain of debt and legal fees with which to deal while raising their four daughters and fighting to keep her ranch.

Harriet tried to earn income with her inventions, but her three patents proved unprofitable. To maintain a cash flow while waiting for the walnut plants to bear walnuts, she developed an innovative process for growing brightly colored pampas plumes that were popular with milliners around the world. Her lucrative plumes business helped her earn enough money to buy more land, which she leased for truck farming. She also drilled three successful oil wells on her property and formed a water company, and her walnut orchards became the largest in the country. She paid all her husband's debts and formidably supported herself and her daughters.

By 1887, Strong became known as the "Walnut Queen," and her irrigation systems became known throughout the southwest. Her inventions of new types of dams and water storage systems represented major breakthroughs in dry land irrigation and helped farmers during the early land settlement of Southern California and much of the southwest. They were widely adopted throughout the region and were credited with speeding the growth of Southern California's food-producing areas. Strong continued developing her ideas for water irrigation and eventually became an advocate for water conservation.

Her campaigns for conservation that helped bring water and electricity to southern California also included flood control innovations that greatly improved the safety and well-being of those living in the flood-prone Los Angeles basin. She invented and patented a flood control/storage dam system that incorporated several dams to serve as "backups" to one another in case of a break.

Strong was an enterprising female engineer who had patents for many different types of dams and water storage systems. By 1890, she had accumulated a substantial fortune, and she began to turn her attention toward societal causes.

Throughout the 1890s, she traveled across the continent with Susan B. Anthony to promote women's suffrage, education, and independence. She became the first female member of the Los Angeles Chamber of Commerce, founded the Ebell Club, was elected the first president of the new feminist Business League of America, and served as a director of the Los Angeles Philharmonic. Strong was the first woman trustee of the University of Southern California Law School and one of the first engineers to advocate diverting water from the Colorado River to Los Angeles.

She appeared before Congress in 1917 to present a plan she designed to control flooding and to help end a dramatic food shortage that had developed during World War I. Her plan was to dam the water of the Colorado River and detour it into a reservoir in the Grand Canyon. Her plan, rejected by the congressional committee for a reason Strong could only determine was that she was female, and she spent the rest of her life fighting for women's rights, as well as for water conservation, farming, and educational improvements.

In 1922, the Reclamation Service presented to Congress a report principally authored by Reclamation Service Chief Arthur Powell Davis calling for development of a hydroelectric power. It would create a reservoir in the Grand Canyon. In 1928, President Calvin Coolidge signed a bill authorizing this project.

In 1929 Harriet Russell Strong died at age eighty-five. In 1931, construction began on the Hoover Dam without reference to her irrefutable groundwork on dam water.

Sources:

Shelby Ellery, "Harriet Russell Strong," *100 Important Women in History*, April 2001, http://www.angelfire.com/anime2/100import/ strong.html; National Women's Hall of Fame, "Harriet Williams Russell Strong," *Women of the Hall*, http://www.womenofthehall. org/inductee/harriet-williams-russell-strong/;

http://www.whittiermuseum.org/Harriet%20Russell%20Strong. html;

http://news.investors.com/management-leaders-and-success/102105-412929-harnessing-the-flow-of-ideas-be-inventive-harriet-russell-strongs-watery-vision-helped-transform-the-arid-west.htm.

August 2010

Chapter Two
Her Quilts Cover and More
∽

Women have always created works of art. But because the painted ceiling barred most women from creating the arts that receive high value in a male society, women channeled their talents into accepted "feminine" artistic expressions, such as needlework and quilts. Quilts did and do exist in fantastic variety wherever there were and are women. They are a universally female art, transcending race, class, national borders, and time.

The art of quilting can be traced back to Syria, Egypt, India, and China, as well as to Europe dating back to the seventeenth century. This art came to America with the first women settlers and slaves. The early American immigrant women from England, Ireland, Germany, and the Netherlands mingled needlework traditions of those countries with new design traditions from the various American Indian tribes. Slave women from Africa made many of the Southern quilts, particularly on large plantations.

American patchwork quilts were first made out of necessity. No factory-made blankets were available in early colonial days, winters were cold, and fabric was scarce as well as expensive. Immigrant men's earnings were meager, and immigrant-slave men's earnings were naught. Industrious women salvaged reusable fabric from worn-out clothes and made blankets called quilts. Albeit a necessity, these pieced-together blankets displayed female artistic expressions through which women could achieve economic, social, and political involvement, particularly in exhibitions at state and county fairs.

Since the work of women quilt makers was not considered "art," women quilters in early colonial days did not encounter the male harassment experienced by most female fine artists. Left in peace, these women oversaw the education and development of their daughters, contributed to women's cultural legacy, and succeeded in their own manner to influence.

Quilting bees became places where women collaborated, making both quilts and history. Though most records claim women at the quilting bees exchanged gossip and recipes, it was obvious to women that was not all that was going on. The fact that Susan B. Anthony made her first speech in Cleveland to women at a church quilting bee gives an indication that then, as always, women had important things to say to each other.

Many women named their quilts with names that bore political or social significance. For example, the Freedom Quilt was given to young men on their twenty-first birthday celebrations. But no comparable quilt celebrated freedom for young women, who were owned by their fathers until marriage and then by their husbands.

Quilts allowed women political expression. At a time when men barred women from voting, women quilters expressed their convictions in a language women understood. In a sense, writes Patricia Mainardi, it was a "secret language." As the story goes, more than one man of Tory political persuasion slept unknowingly under his wife's Whig Rose quilt. In the Radical Rose design of the Civil War period, each rose had a black center to express empathy with the slaves. It has been suggested there were quilts that bore signals communicating with slaves who could not read, hung over fences or clotheslines by courageous women guiding the men and women on the Underground Railroad to "safe" houses.

Historically, quilts have been excluded from art literature, art history, and art museums. But in 2002 the Museum of Fine Arts, Houston, sponsored an exhibit of the Quilts of Gee's Bend. A second Gee's Bend quilt exhibit, organized in 2006, toured seven other city museums, including the Indianapolis Museum of Art and the Orlando Museum of Art (January 27–May 13, 2007).

Sources:

Patricia Mainardi, *Quilts: The Great American Art* (San Pedro: California, Miles & Weir, Ltd., 1978.

Joanne Cubbs, Dana Friis-Hansen, and Matt Arnett, *Mary Lee Bendolph, Gee's Bend Quilts, and Beyond* (Atlanta: Tinwood Books, 2006).

Amy Crawford, "An Interview with Amei Wallach, author of 'Fabric of Their Lives,'" *Smithsonian.com*, September 30, 2006, http://www.smithsonianmag.com/arts-culture/an-interview-with-amei-wallach-author-of-fabric-of-their-lives-134194216/#hijQhqDIyl6cuCVb.99.

December 2003

Chapter Three
Legal Age and Sex Discrimination
~

*I*n the double discrimination case of Jones v. University of Manchester (1993), Ms. Jones, age 46, was denied consideration for a post as a career adviser at the University of Manchester because she did not meet the preferred age requirement of twenty-five to thirty-five with varied work experience.

Ms. Jones asserted the requirement process was indirectly discriminatory on grounds of sex. She alleged the relevant pool of possible applicants for comparison was of mature students aged twenty-five or above. Statistical evidence demonstrated that, although the proportion of male mature students aged twenty-five to twenty-nine was greater than that of female mature students, in the group of mature students aged thirty and over, the proportion of female mature students was greater.

Arguments demonstrated the gender/age imbalance included the "historical reason" that women, in general, were not offered opportunities in accordance with their abilities. Thus, they were unable to progress to levels of higher education equal to those of men.

Her argument included the "family reason" that assigns women in their early twenties to the role of having children and then, because of their family commitments, makes them unable to pursue a university degree until their children have reached, at least, school age. Ms. Jones was victorious. However, the decision was reversed in a higher court.

The US Age Discrimination in Employment Act of 1967 generally prohibits employers from discriminating against workers or applicants forty years of age or over and, specifically, between the ages of forty and sixty-five.

A most memorable age and sex discrimination case in the United States involving a female in a male-dominated industry (electronic journalism) is that of Christine Craft. In 1981 Ms. Craft had been demoted from anchor to reporter by her bosses at KMBC-TV in Kansas City, Missouri, because she was "too old, too ugly, not deferential to men." Craft, then thirty-seven, sued for sexual discrimination and won, only to lose on appeal.

Source:

https://en.wikipedia.org/wiki/Jones_v_University_of_Manchester. January 2004

Chapter Four
Female Pharaohs to Fathom
~

*I*n the millennium before the birth of Jesus, it was women who ran the most important temple in the nation, possibly in the world, the Karnak temple in Thebes. Thus, Cleopatra, as a strong and intelligent woman running a major country, was nothing new. She was simply the latest in a line of important Ptolemaic queens, among them Hatshepsut and Nefertiti.

Hatshepsut was quite dismissed in biased history books authored by nineteenth century male scholars. Though she was written to be a pacifist who never did anything for the country, Hatshepsut expanded the empire; restored and built temples; led the Egyptian army into the Sudan, a land coveted for its gold; and oversaw at least three other military campaigns. Nefertiti ruled with her husband Amenhotep IV, who decreed that Egyptians worship a single deity, the sun disk. Nefertiti was the high priestess of this new religion. The sun cult died with Amenhotep, and Nefertiti dropped from historical sight.

Egypt was rich in gold, grain, and ships but had become a third-rate power by the time Cleopatra came to power in 55 BC at age eighteen. The politically astute Cleopatra knew that, to make her mark in a Roman world, she needed to befriend rather than alienate Roman leaders.

Under her rule, Egypt was the only Mediterranean nation independent of Romans. In her relations with Caesar, politics and love seem to have been interfused. Caesar almost always involved himself with women who could advance him politically. At fifty-two, he realized Cleopatra, then twenty-one, as his lover and confidant, would make both him and Rome a valuable ally. To judge by extant portraits, Cleopatra was not really beautiful, yet she must have enthralled Caesar. Perchance what enthralled him was the politics of charm, which became the charm of politics.

Perhaps Mark Antony was drawn to Cleopatra because she had many of the personal leadership qualities he sorely lacked. During the time they were allied, she administered Egypt alone, and evidence suggests she was a caring, capable, and efficient ruler who managed the economy well and treated her people justly.

During her reign, in contrast to those of her predecessors, there were no rebellions, and tax collection proceeded normally. She improved and expanded agriculture, producing large surpluses of grain, eliminating food shortages, and lowering food prices. She was a highly educated woman who became fluent in Demotic Egyptian, the local language of the people. Sources claim she spoke eight languages.

After Antony died, Octavian sent soldiers to take Cleopatra into custody. His plans included marching this "treacherous creature" in chains through the streets of Rome, showing what would happen to women who did not know their place in the Roman world. She decided to rob him of that satisfaction and took her own life.

In her thirty-nine years, twenty-one as Egypt's queen, Cleopatra demonstrated no less intelligence, political skills, sheer courage, and audacity than the powerful male leaders with whom she had dealt. She used her wiles not so much for herself but to protect her beloved Egypt.

In a propaganda speech against her, Octavian spoke of how the Romans viewed any woman who had the gall to think she could assume the "manly" role of ruling a country. In the end, they and their totally male-dominated system devoured her. Folklore emphasized how she lived and died for love, but Cleopatra was one of the major politicians in world history. She stood for and dreamed of a world in which men and women might meet on an even playing field.

Sources:

Janet Johnson professor of Egyptology at the University of Chicago's Oriental Institute. Barbara Lesko in *Women in World History Encyclopedia*; *Cleopatra,* ed. Don Nardo.

Chicago Tribune: William Mullen http://articles.chicagotribune.com/2001-06-28/news/0106280224_1_cleopatra-british-museum-field-museum 6/28/01.

Barbara Brotman http://articles.chicagotribune.com/2001-11-14/features/0111140119_1_egypt-cleopatra-ordinary-women 11/14/01.

http://articles.chicagotribune.com/keyword/cleopatra/featured/2.

http://articles.chicagotribune.com/2002-02-03/news/0202030046_1_antony-and-cleopatra-marc-antony-pharaonic-egypt James Philips 2/3/02.

November 2004

Chapter Five
First American Black Woman's Bank
~

*H*er mother was a slave, her biological Irish father had been a Confederate soldier and, after the Civil War, was a Southern correspondent for the *New York Herald*. But it was 1864, and interracial marriages were illegal in Virginia. Thus, Elizabeth Draper married William Mitchell, a mulatto man who could pass as the father of ten-month-old Maggie Lena.

When Maggie was a toddler, William Mitchell disappeared and was found drowned. It was assumed he had been robbed and murdered. To support her family, Elizabeth took in laundry. As Maggie grew, she helped to deliver the clean clothes. She attended school, graduated with honors in 1883, and taught at her alma mater for three years while studying accounting at night. She dreamed of founding a bank owned and operated by African Americans, albeit she lived in an era when women could neither vote nor own property, with slavery newly abolished.

In 1886, Maggie married building contractor Armstead Walker, bore him three children, and charted her career. She joined the Independent Order of St. Luke, an African American fraternal society established in 1867 in Baltimore that administered to the sick and aged, promoted humanitarian causes and encouraged individual self-help and integrity. Walker worked up the ranks in the Order and was elected its Right Worthy Grand Secretary and Treasurer at its 1899 convention. Because the Order was in debt, she accepted the position at one-third the salary, or eight dollars a month. She enacted programs under which the Order financially prospered. She traveled to organize new councils, and her speaking abilities brought new membership.

Through her business-savvy innovations, Maggie diversified the Order to include an insurance component, a printing press, a newspaper, an educational loan fund for college students, and a juvenile branch for the youth. She also established an Order newsletter, with a section devoted just to children. She encouraged the young to save money and set up a "Sunshine Day," when they would visit the sick and/or take food to families in need.

Her dream of founding a bank was still alive. She believed her people could turn their nickels into dollars by pooling their money and lending it out. She said, "Let us put our money together; let us use our money; let us put our money out at usury among ourselves and reap the benefits ourselves."

On November 2, 1903, Maggie Lena Walker became the first black woman bank founder and president in the United States when the St. Luke Penny Savings Bank opened with opening day receipts of $9,430.44. Many people started Christmas savings accounts, in which they deposited a penny or a nickel every week. Her bank prospered. But in 1911, a new Virginia law required all banks to separate from fraternal organizations. Despite the new law, her bank continued to succeed, and by 1920, it had helped to purchase six hundred homes.

In 1929, Maggie met with officers and directors for the Second Street Savings Bank and Commercial Bank and Trust to discuss a merger. The Commercial Bank and Trust dropped out of discussions, and the two remaining banks adopted a resolution to merge. The new institution, the Consolidated Bank and Trust, opened for business on January 2, 1930, at the First and Marshall Street location of the St. Luke Penny Savings Bank. The Commercial Bank and Trust, still facing financial troubles in 1931, merged with Consolidated.

Walker was appointed chairman of the board of directors for Consolidated Bank and Trust, a position she held until her death in 1934. While many banks did not survive the Great Depression, Consolidated Bank and Trust, with assets over $116 million, thrived until 2009, when it was bought by the Premier Bank, ending it's distinction as a black-run, independently owned bank. It is believed to have been the oldest continuously black-owned bank in the United States.

As segregation in the South increased under Jim Crow laws, black entrepreneurship campaigns such as "buy black" of the 1960s developed. Walker added a powerful plea for the employment of black women in other than domestic service. Walker became a philanthropist and increasingly active in civic affairs and charities. She founded and was the lifelong head of the Colored Women's Council of Richmond, which supported the Janie Porter Barrett Virginian Industrial School for Colored Girls.

Walker was a member of the National Urban League, the Virginia Interracial Committee, the National Association of Wage Earners, and the International Council of Women of the Darker Races. She was cofounder and vice president of the Richmond branch of the NAACP, and served for many years on the executive committee of the National Association of Colored Women. She served on the board of two schools for girls and as a trustee of Hartshorn College and Virginia Union University.

Walker received an honorary master's degree from Virginia Union University in 1923. In her honor, Richmond Public Schools built Maggie L. Walker High School adjacent to Virginia Union University. It was one of Richmond's two schools for black students during the period of racial segregation in schools. It was refurbished in the late twentieth century to become the regional Maggie L. Walker Governor's School for Government and International Studies. *Newsweek* magazine lists it as one of the top public elite schools in the nation. In 2002, Walker was inducted into the Junior Achievement U.S. Business Hall of Fame.

As Walker aged, her health declined. Though confined to a wheelchair in 1928 due to paralysis, Walker remained active, serving as leader of the Order and chairman of the bank until her death in 1934.

The Maggie L. Walker Historical Site, designated a national historic site in 1978, opened as a museum in 1985. It commemorates the life of the female bank founder and president of the first black woman's bank.

Sources:

http://www.nps.gov/mawa/learn/historyculture/index.htm

http://www.encyclopediavirginia.org/Maggie_Lena_Walker_1864-1934

http://www.nps.gov/mawa/the-st-luke-penny-savings-bank.htm.

Watch video: https://www.youtube.com/watch?v=SBuDSLrRKBU

February 2009

Chapter Six
Counting Women of Color

 L ess than 1 percent of all mathematicians are black. Of these, 25 percent are women. In the early half of the twentieth century, many black women obtained master's degrees in mathematics, but not until 1943 was the first PhD in mathematics bestowed upon an African American woman.

Euphemia Lofton Haynes earned her master's in education at the University of Chicago in 1930 and became the first African American woman to earn a PhD in mathematics at Catholic University in Washington, DC. Dr. Haynes taught in DC public schools for forty-seven years and was the first woman to chair the DC School Board. At Miners Teacher's College in the District, Dr. Haynes established the mathematics department and served as its chair.

The second African American woman to earn a PhD in mathematics was Evelyn Boyd Granville at Yale University in 1949. The third African American woman to earn a PhD in mathematics was Marjorie Lee Browne in 1950 at the University of Michigan. Argelia Velez-Rodriguez became the fourth African American women to earn a PhD in mathematics in 1960 at the University of Havana.

Georgia Caldwell Smith passed her PhD defense in 1960. Due to her death, her PhD was conferred posthumously in 1961 the year Sadie Gasaway became the fifth African American woman to earn a PhD in mathematics at Cornell. The sixth, Lillian K. Bradley, also was the first black woman to earn a doctorate in any field at the University of Texas when she earned her DEd in mathematics education. This is important to note because of the racist attitudes in the University of Texas Mathematics Department.

The seventh and eighth African American women to earn PhDs in mathematics were Gloria Conyers Hewitt (University of Washington in Seattle) and Louise Nixon Sutton (New York University), both in 1962. In 1963, Grace Lele Williams became the first African (Nigerian) woman to earn any doctorate when she got her PhD in mathematics at the University of Chicago. In 1965, the ninth and tenth African American women to earn PhDs in mathematics were Beryl Eleanor Hunte (New York University) and Thyrsa Frazier Svager (Ohio State).

In 1966, the eleventh, twelfth, and thirteenth African American women earned their PhDs in mathematics. They were Eleanor Dawley Jones at Syracuse University, Shirley Mathis McBay at the University of Georgia, and Vivienne Malone Mayes. Mayes was the first African American woman to earn a PhD in any field at the University of Texas at Austin, despite the difficulties African Americans who attempted to earn degrees in the South prior to 1970 faced.

In 1967, Geraldine Darden was the fourteenth African American woman to earn a PhD in mathematics (Syracuse University). In 1968, Mary Lovenia DeConge-Watson was the fifteenth African American woman to earn a PhD in mathematics (St. Louis University). And in 1969, Etta Zuba Falconer was the sixteenth African American woman to earn a PhD in mathematics (Emory).

The seventeenth African American woman to earn a PhD in mathematics was Genevieve Knight (math education, University of Maryland) in 1970. The following year, Joella H. Gipson (University of Illinois) and Dolores Spikes (Louisiana State) became the eighteenth and nineteenth African American women to earn PhDs in mathematics.

In 1972, at Ohio State, Rada Higgins McCreadie was the twentieth African American woman to earn a PhD in mathematics. Also in this year, Prince Winston Armstrong earned her DEd in mathematics from the University of Oklahoma.

In 1992, Gloria Gilmer was the first African American woman to deliver a major National Association of Mathematicians (NAM) lecture.

Kate Okikiolu was the first black to win mathematics' most prestigious young person's award, the Sloan Research Fellowship in 1997. She also was awarded the new $500,000 Presidential Early Career Awards for Scientists and Engineers.

In 2000, three African American women earned PhDs in one year when the University of Maryland graduated its first mathematics women PhDs—Tasha Inniss, Sherry Scott, and Kimberly Weems. In 2001, Kate Okikiolu became the first black woman to publish in the mathematics journal, *The Annals of Mathematics*. Counting women of color counts.

Sources:
> http://www.math.buffalo.edu/mad/wohist.html.
> http://www.math.buffalo.edu/mad/wmad0.html.
> http://www.math.buffalo.edu/mad/madhist.html.

February 2008

Chapter Seven
First Lady of the Black Press
~

S he both reported on and experienced black history as it was being made. She suffered verbal and physical abuse from segregationists. She recalled an angry mob that confronted her in Selma during the early civil rights movement, how she could feel the hatred and would never forget the contorted faces of the people screaming racial slurs in her face.

The granddaughter of slaves, Ethel L. Payne was born in Chicago in 1911, the fifth of six children. Her mother was a high school Latin teacher, and her father, a Pullman porter. Little has been written about her early years, but it is known that she attended Lindblom High School and Crane Jr. College. She wanted to be a civil rights lawyer, but was not accepted into law school, and searched for a profession while working as a clerk at the Chicago Public Library.

In 1948, Payne left Chicago to take a position with the Red Cross as director of a special forces army club in Japan. It was there her writing talents were discovered quite by chance. She kept a journal detailing her experiences and observations, many of which focused on the black soldiers and their experiences in the primarily white armed forces.

At a press club in downtown Tokyo, Payne met with other correspondents, some who had come during the Korean conflict. She shared her journal notes with one of them, Alex Wilson. Wilson was a reporter for the *Chicago Defender*, a black newspaper founded specifically to publish issues in the black community that were not covered in white newspapers. Wilson liked what he read and asked if he could publish her writings. Payne agreed and saw her career in journalism begin.

The *Defender* ran her stories of black troops stationed in Japan on its front page, publicity perhaps not welcomed by the US military, and offered Payne a job doing feature articles. She accepted the offer, returned to the United States in 1951, and bylined with accomplished writers, such as William Motley, Gwendolyn Brooks, and Langston Hughes, who also wrote for the *Defender*. After joining the paper, Payne earned a degree from Medill School of Journalism at Northwestern University.

Her first piece won first prize at the Illinois Press Association. Payne's articles on civil rights were piercing and straightforward, as was Payne, who was living the civil rights issues about which she was reporting. Payne was moved to investigative reporting, and the *Defender*'s editor offered her a position as the paper's correspondent in its Washington, DC bureau. She was one of three black journalists in the White House Press Corps in the 1950s, when racial discrimination was just beginning to be reported on a national level. But not so fast.

President Dwight David Eisenhower held weekly press conferences. At one conference in 1954, the president called on Payne. Their encounter resulted in the national spotlight on Payne and civil rights. Her question to Eisenhower concerned the recent decision of the Interstate Commerce Commission to end segregation practices on interstate highways. She asked of his plans to initiate the commission's decision. Eisenhower was noticeably uncomfortable by her question and sternly informed her that he would be fair but would not cater to special interests. But to Payne, desegregation of black American citizens did not qualify as a special interest.

Following reports that Payne was disruptive, *The Washington Post* reported, "She was not 'trying to make waves' but rather to find out when and how the powers might act to end racial discrimination in housing, interstate travel and other areas in which government might act." Eisenhower did not recognize Payne at future press conferences.

But Payne also covered stories overseas. She was the first black woman journalist to focus on international news reporting heavily promoted in the *Defender*. Her journalism took her to the Asian-African Conference in Bandung, Indonesia, and she covered Ghana's independence movement.

In 1966, she was assigned to cover the black troops fighting in the Vietnam War. For three months, Payne reported from Vietnam. She went into the field, observed where soldiers learned guerrilla warfare, investigated American military supplies being sold on the black market, and witnessed the death of a Vietnamese woman. During the latter, she experienced firsthand the effects of Agent Orange. After the Vietnam War, she traveled to Nigeria to cover the Nigerian Civil War, to Mexico to cover the International Women's Year Conference in Mexico City, and to Africa on separate occasions with Secretaries of State William P. Rogers and Henry Kissinger.

She became the first black woman to be employed by a national network as a radio and television commentator when offered a job with CBS's *Spectrum*. After six years, she moved to the WBBM program *Matters of Opinion*, where she stayed until 1982. Her commentary always discussed topics important to the African American community—in essence, to the entire American community.

In 1972, she became an associate editor at the *Defender*. Six years later, after twenty-eight years with the newspaper, she returned to Washington to pursue her interest in international news and began a syndicated column that ran in six black newspapers nationwide. But because she was a woman, evidenced perhaps even in the circle of the black male-dominated media, she and journalist Alfreda L. Madison were unable to secure tickets to a 1987 Black Caucus dinner representing the black media. Later, caucus leaders cited outrage for this gender disparate treatment against two women who had opened doors for many black women (and men, but especially women) in journalism.

Upon her passing in 1991 at the age of eighty, *The Washington Post* wrote, "Had Ethel Payne not been black, she certainly would have been one of the most recognized journalists in American society." That said and written, Ethel L. Payne, who did not start out to be a journalist, is recognized as the "first lady of the black press."

Sources:

Darlene Clark Hine, ed., *Black Women in America: Business and Professions*, 1997.

Genise Clark. "Ethel L. Payne, Early Journalist," *The Newark Metro*, http://www.newarkmetro.rutgers.edu/essays/display.php?id=236

James McGrath Morris, "Ethel Payne, 'First Lady of the Black Press,' Asked Questions No One Else Would," *The Washington Post*, August 12, 2011, http://www.washingtonpost.com/opinions/ethel-paynefirst-lady-of-the-black-pressasked-questions-no-one-else-would/2011/08/02/gIQAJloFBJ_story.html.

Suggested reading:

James McGrath Morris, *Eye on the Struggle: Ethel Payne the First Lady of the Black Press.*

February 2012

Chapter Eight
NAACP White Woman Founder
~

M ary White Ovington (1865–1951) moved a country. Born into a wealthy abolitionist family two years after the Emancipation Proclamation ended slavery, she attended a prestigious girls' school in Brooklyn, then Harvard Annex, now Radcliffe College. As a young woman, she helped found Brooklyn's Greenpoint Settlement in 1895 and worked there without remuneration until 1903 to improve conditions for the working class. She joined the Social Reform Club, where she became aware through Booker T. Washington that racism existed in the North, and not only in the South. This transformed her. She had never thought of Negroes as a separate class.

She began to study the status of Negroes in the North. She investigated their housing conditions, their health, and their opportunities for employment (or lack thereof). She interacted with the many educated Negroes in New York and learned from them about issues of racial discrimination, specifically educational and enfranchisement roadblocks put up by whites. She decided her future reform work would focus on improving conditions for colored people.

In 1904, Ovington met W.E.B. Du Bois of Harvard, and they began a dialogue centered on social reform. She supported his work through fundraisers, and as a reporter for the *New York Evening Post*, she promoted and publicized his efforts to end racial discrimination in America. She grew to believe that something major had to be done—something that would move the country.

Ovington was part of the Cosmopolitan Club, a group of about thirty black and white citizens who, since 1906, had been meeting in private homes to discuss improved race relations. In 1908, she organized a public meeting in a New York restaurant. The meeting was considered scandalous, and unfavorable press coverage nationwide cursed her.

That summer, race riots exploded and raged for days in Springfield, Illinois, home of the great emancipator Abraham Lincoln. Lynching and violence in Springfield's streets shocked and shook the country, as mobs of white people, many of them distinguished citizens, killed and wounded hundreds of black people and drove thousands from the city.

Multiple articles about the riots appeared in newspapers and magazines far beyond the boundaries of Illinois. One in the *Independent* titled "Race War in the North" by William Walling, himself a white man, described atrocities by whites committed against colored people.

Walling's article called for the revival of the spirit of the abolitionists. He wrote that the Negro must be treated on a plane of absolute political and social equality or the war on race would transfer to the North. He ended his article with a seemingly unanswerable hypothetical question: "Yet who realizes the seriousness of the situation, and what large and powerful body of citizens is ready to come to their [the Negro's] aid?"

The article reached Ovington, who was living in a New York Negro tenement after months of having lived in the South. Her surroundings, her investigations, her interracial experiences, her abolitionist roots, and now these riots confirmed her belief that something of major proportion had to be done to move the country. She realized the seriousness of the situation Walling had written about, and she had an answer to his hypothetical question. Ovington wrote to Walling.

Walling did not respond for some time. When he did, they met in New York the first week of January 1909. Dr. Henry Moskowitz, a white man in the administration of the New York City mayor's office, joined them. Oblivious of what was to come, no minutes were recorded.

In a small New York City apartment, in the midst of rampant racial unrest, groundwork to establish what was to become the NAACP began. And, it began as an interracial organization led by a white woman of privilege, conviction, and courage when Ovington proposed the formation of a stalwart, nationwide, interracial organization. After she cited her studies, investigations, and knowledge about unjust treatment of Negroes in the North, the meeting ended with a formal "call" for a national conference to discuss her proposal.

The "call" was signed by sixty influential people most of them from Ovington's inner circle. Sixteen were women, four from Chicago's Hull House women, Jane Addams, Florence Kelley, Mary McDowell, and Lillian Wald—and also Ida B. Wells Others included Du Bois, Moskowitz, Walling, Wm. Lloyd Garrison, and Francis Grimke. All but Wells, Grimke, and Du Bois were white.

A committee was formed from these supporters, and a National Negro Conference was held in New York City later that same year. The following year, at a second conference, the organization was formalized and named the National Association for the Advancement of Colored People (NAACP). Ovington's efforts assured that over a third of the organization's members were women and arranged for black women to have active roles.

Throughout a tumultuous period of attempting to organize an uncharted black and white endeavor, Ovington worked tirelessly. She was the chief fund-raiser and conference organizer, and she traveled the country recruiting supporters and starting local branches. She served as board member, executive secretary, and chairwoman. Most of her contributions were unpublicized.

Honored by the board in 1931 as the "Mother of the New Emancipation," Ovington continued her work until 1947, when poor health and her eighty-two years of age left her unable serve as the white woman founder of the NAACP, who moved a country.

Sources:

Black and White Sat Down Together: The Reminiscences of an NAACP Founder, Ralph Luker

Freedom's Daughters: The Unsung Heroines of the Civil Rights Movement from 1830 to 1970, Lynne Olson

http://www.pointsoflight.org/programs/recognition/extra-mile/mary-white-ovington-and-william-edward-burghardt-web-dubois.

NAACP 100 Celebrating a Century 100 Years in Pictures, Gibbs Smith
   Press.

http://www.naacp.org/pages/naacp-history-Mary-White-Ovington.
September 2009

Chapter Nine
Presidential Convention Women
~

*T*he first female US presidential candidate appeared on the scene in 1872 when abolitionist and suffragist, Victoria Woodhull was nominated by the newly formed Equal Rights Party as its US presidential nominee. Frederick Douglass declined to be VP on her ticket.

The second woman to run, Belva Ann Bennett Lockwood (1830–1917), a DC attorney who was the first woman member of the US Supreme Court Bar and the first woman lawyer to argue before the Supreme Court. Lockwood ran as the Equal Rights candidate in 1884 and 1888. Her vice presidential running mate, the first female VP candidate, was Marietta Lizzie Bell Stowe.

Lockwood received about 4,100 votes (thirty-five years before women were allowed to cast their votes) and petitioned the United States Congress to have her ballots counted. She claimed supporters had seen their ballots ripped up, that she had received one-half the electoral vote of Oregon and a large vote in Pennsylvania not counted but rather dumped into the wastebasket. Albeit a woman of exceptional credentials, *The Atlanta Constitution* labeled her "old lady Lockwood," not a presumptive "Madame President." In 1892, Woodhull again ran for president, the last woman to run for another seventy-two years.

At the 1964 Republican National Convention, Senator Margaret Chase Smith (R-Maine) was nominated for president and received twenty-seven votes on the floor, but the nomination went to Barry Goldwater. Eight years later, at the 1972 Democratic National Convention, US Representative Shirley Chisholm (D-New York) ran for the US presidency. Chisholm, the first African American woman elected to Congress (1968), received 152 votes on the floor, but the nomination went to Senator George McGovern. Also that year, in the Oregon presidential primary, Congresswoman Patsy Takemoto Mink (D-Hawaii) ran for the US presidency. Mink, the first Asian American woman elected to Congress (1965) was author of Title IX (1972).

Ellen McCormack's name appeared on the ballot in eighteen states as a candidate for the Democratic Party's presidential nomination in 1976. She was the first female candidate to have raised enough money to qualify for federal matching funds. She ran as a housewife on a pro-life platform and received Secret Service protection during her campaign. She did not win any primaries but engaged in a debate that included future President Jimmy Carter. She had her name placed into nomination at the Democratic National Convention and received twenty-two delegate votes. In 1980, McCormack ran as a third-party candidate and received 32,327 votes.

In the 1984 election, Sonia Johnson ran and received 72,161 votes as the presidential candidate of the US Citizens Party. In that same year, Democratic nominee Walter Mondale chose former US Representative Geraldine Ferraro (D-New York) as his running mate.

US Representative Pat Schroeder (D-Colorado) entered the presidential race late in 1988 when Gary Hart withdrew after his marital infidelities became public. Having raised just under $850,000 of the $2 million she projected she needed, Schroeder withdrew her candidacy.

Lenora Branch Fulani, an American psychologist, also ran in 1988 on the New Alliance Party ticket. Fulani was the first woman and the first African American with ballot access in all fifty states, as well as the first African American female candidate who raised enough money to qualify for federal matching funds. Fulani received .2 percent of the vote, more than any woman in history. Her platform included racial equality, gay rights, and political reform. She ran again in 1992.

After a long career in politics, first as a Democrat and then as a Republican, Elizabeth Dole ran for the Republican nomination in 2000. Dole pulled out of the race before any of the primaries, largely due to inadequate fundraising.

The first female African American US Senator, Carol Moseley Braun (D-Illinois), campaigned for the Democratic Party nomination in 2004. Moseley Braun raised little money and withdrew before the Iowa caucuses.

Former First Lady Senator Hillary Rodham Clinton (D-New York) entered the 2008 US presidential campaign. Her New Hampshire victory marked the first time a woman had ever won a primary. Clinton won eighteen primaries and garnered almost eighteen million votes. Her name was placed into nomination at the Democratic National Convention in Denver, Colorado where she moved that Barack Obama be selected as the Democratic Party's 2008 presidential nominee by acclamation, making Obama the first African American to receive a major party's presidential nomination.

The next week, at the Republican National Convention in St. Paul, Minnesota, Alaska Governor Sarah Palin was named as presidential nominee John McCain's running mate.

Sources:

Mary L. Shearer, "Who Is Victoria Woodhull?" *Victoria Woodhull, the Spirit to Run the White House*, October 27, 1999, http://www.victoria-woodhull.com/whoisvw.htm.

National Women's History Museum, "Lenora Fulani," NWHM cyber exhibit "Women Who Ran for President," https://www.nwhm.org/education-resources/biography/biographies/lenora-fulani/; http://www.nysl.nysed.gov/msscfa/sc21041.htm; https://en.wikipedia.org/wiki/List_of_female_United_States_presidential_and_vice-presidential_candidates;

Wikipedia for each woman named.

September 2008

Chapter Ten
Madam Mayors

~

Susanna Madora Salter was the first woman ever elected mayor in any American city. The city was Argonia, Kansas, a little Quaker village with a population of less than five hundred. The year was 1887 the same year Kansas allowed women to vote. Some in Argonia deemed politics the exclusive domain of men and resented the inclusion of women. A backroom caucus was convened and a scheme put in place supposedly to, teach these women a lesson. But the women in question learned of the scheme and navigated it as best they could. Salter won, with two-thirds of the vote. She made Argonia famous and women proud, nationally and internationally.

Alice Kerr was the first woman to serve as mayor of Edmonds, Washington, having beaten the incumbent, whose victory had been a foregone conclusion in the 1924 election, with a final tally of 163–159. Kerr had moved from Chicago to Edmonds in 1920. At the time of her death in 1949, she was the first and only woman to have served as mayor of Edmonds.

Bertha Knight Landes became the first woman mayor of a major American city after her election as mayor of Seattle in 1926. Her campaign platform of "municipal housekeeping" aimed to clean up city government. Landes had not voted until just six years previous, when passage of the nineteenth amendment to the Constitution allowed her to exercise her right to vote. In her 1928 bid for reelection, Landes received endorsements from all of Seattle's major newspapers, the Central Labor Council, the Prohibition Party, and women's organizations. But she lost to a male who was politically unknown. Landis attributed her defeat in great measure to "sex prejudice." Landes was the last female mayor of Seattle.

Unita Blackwell, in 1976, became the first African American woman to be elected mayor in Mississippi. In 1964, Blackwell, a daughter of sharecroppers, and seven other blacks went to the Mayersville courthouse to register to vote and encountered vehement opposition by white farmers. The racism the group experienced that day was the "turning point" of Blackwell's life, and she began organizing voter drives across Mississippi. She joined Fannie Lou Hamer's delegation at the 1964 Democratic National Convention in an attempt to get blacks seated as delegates. In the late 1960s, she worked with the National Council of Negro Women and was jailed over seventy times. As mayor, Blackwell became a voice for rural housing and development. She oversaw the construction of federal public housing, the first to be built in Issaquena County. In 1982 at age forty-nine, Blackwell received a master's degree in regional planning.

Dianne Feinstein as president of the board of supervisors of San Francisco succeeded to the city's mayoralty in 1978, when Dan White assassinated San Francisco Mayor George Moscone and Supervisor Harvey Milk at city hall. Feinstein was elected in her own right in 1979 and reelected to a second full term in 1983. Feinstein, a centrist, angered the city's large gay community by refusing to march in a gay rights parade and by vetoing domestic partner legislation in 1983. In 1984, Feinstein proposed banning handguns in San Francisco and became subject to a recall attempt. She won the recall election and completed her second mayoral term. In 1987, *City & State* magazine named Feinstein the nation's "Most Effective Mayor."

In 1979, Jane Margaret Byrne became the first and, to date, only woman to hold the office of mayor in Chicago, thus she made Chicago the largest city in the United States to elect a woman to this high office. As mayor, Byrne hired the first black school superintendent and moved into the crime-ridden public housing development of Cabrini-Green for a short but highly publicized period to bring attention and resources to the high crime rate there. Cabrini-Green was permanently shuttered and scheduled for demolition in 2010. Byrne was the first Chicago mayor to recognize the gay community, and she effectively banned handgun possession in the city for guns unregistered or purchased after the enactment of an ordinance. She is responsible for the direct "L" lines from the city to both Chicago airports. On July 4, 1980, Mayor Byrne blocked off Michigan Avenue for the first Taste of Chicago. Taste moved to Grant Park the next year and has been held there every year hence.

Jessie Menifield Rattley was the first woman to be elected mayor of Newport News, Virginia, in 1986. Her previous 1970 election as the first African American elected to the Newport News City Council was a major turning point in the civil rights movement for residents of the city's Southeast community (mostly African Americans) who witnessed funding for their schools and city services increased. During her tenure as mayor, Rattley received some criticism from residents due to her controversial plan to expand HUD and federally subsidized, low-income housing into what were the more upscale sections of the city. Still, in 2005, the Newport News City Hall and the government buildings immediately surrounding it were rededicated the Jessie Menifield Rattley Municipal Center in her honor.

Carrie Saxon Perry, elected mayor of Hartford, Connecticut in 1987, was the first black woman to head a large US city. Political parity was, and always had been, the focus and the force of Perry's political career. She believed in political parity at all levels of government to provide a voice for blacks and women.

This sampling of women mayors elected in the one hundred years from 1887 to 1987 represents a century of past political progress as political gender parity still looms to be futuristic.

Sources:

Monroe Billington, "Susanna Madora Salter: First Woman Mayor," *Kansas Collection: Kansas Historical Quarterlies*, http://www.kancoll.org/khq/1954/54_3_billington.htm.

Mildred Andrews, "Landes, Bertha Knight (1868–1943)," HistoryLink.org, March 2, 2003, http://www.historylink.org/index.cfm?DisplayPage=output.cfm&File_Id=5343

My Edmonds News, "This Month in Edmonds History: Alice Kerr becomes Town's First Woman Mayor," January 1, 2011, http://myedmondsnews.com/2011/01/this-month-in-edmonds-history-in-1925-alice-kerr-becomes-towns-first-mayor/.

Hal Dardick, "Water Tower Park to Be Renamed for Jane Byrne," *Chicago Tribune*, July 29, 2014, http://www.chicagotribune.com/news/politics/clout/chi-water-tower-park-to-be-be-renamed-for-jane-byrne-20140729,0,2665433.story.

February 2011

Chapter Eleven
Start the/Her Presses
~

*E*lizabeth Glover established America's first printing press business in 1638 in Cambridge, Massachusetts. As a woman without a husband, the widow Glover needed special permission from male government officials to open her business. She continued to manage the Cambridge Press during her second marriage to Henry Dunster, Harvard's first president. After his death in 1654, Glover turned over the business to Harvard College.

Another widow, Dinah Nuthead, became the first licensed female printing operator in the colonies in 1686. It is believed she was illiterate.

In 1738, Elizabeth Timothy was the colonies' first female newspaper publisher and editor. Timothy printed the *South Carolina Gazette* in partnership with Ben Franklin, who owned the press and founded the newspaper. As a woman, she operated under her thirteen-year-old son's name, Peter.

The fourth newspaper in the colonies was the *American Weekly Mercury*, published by Cornelia Bradford after the death of her husband. When Bradford sold the paper, she continued to work as a bookbinder and printer.

Lydia Maria Francis published America's first children's magazine, *Juvenile Miscellany*, in 1826. Francis had written her first book at age twenty-two. It was a daring romance between a Native American man and a white woman. After her marriage to David Child, she wrote *The Frugal Housewife*, the first of such books, in 1829 America. Her *History of the Condition of Women* followed in 1837. She then wrote another first book of its kind, in which she argued against slavery. And in 1841, she edited the *National Anti-Slavery Standard*. Subsequently, subscriptions to her children's magazine were canceled, numerous by "respectable" Bostonians.

The domineering husband of Jane Grey Swisshelm forbade her to read. But read she did, as well as write and even publish. She published newspapers in three different cities, one of them Pittsburgh. Under Pennsylvania law, a woman's wages went to her husband. When Swisshelm learned he could make money from (his wife) Jane's writings, he allowed her to launch her own paper, the *Pittsburgh Saturday Visiter*, where her editorials on slavery had a national audience of abolitionists. In 1850, she became the first woman to sit in the press gallery of the United States Senate. In 1857, she left her husband, moved to Minnesota, and published the *St. Cloud Visiter*, in which she continued to write against slavery. After pro-slavery advocates destroyed her press, she restarted her paper as the *St. Cloud Democrat*.

Maria Stewart was America's first African American journalist. Her abolitionist essays of 1831–33 were published in William Lloyd Garrison's newspaper, *The Liberator*. The male leaders of the free-black community, however, were intolerant of a publicly outspoken female journalist. Stewart was forced to leave Boston and her career. Stewart's essays and speeches were collected and preserved in a 1987 anthology edited by Marilyn Richardson.

The first African American newspaper publisher in America was Mary Ann Shadd Cary. Born free in Philadelphia in 1823, Cary became a teacher. At age twenty-seven, when Congress passed the 1850 Fugitive Slave Law, Cary and her family fled to Canada. There she established *The Provincial Freeman*, a weekly publication for other blacks living in Canada. Criticism from black men made it difficult for her to publish. But publish she did. Their resistance didn't stop her.

In 1892, Ida B. Wells, owner of the *Memphis Free Speech* newspaper, wrote an editorial urging blacks to move out of racially restrictive Memphis. Within two months, six thousand had done just that. Wells observed that many of the young, black men being lynched were those who were making economic gains in their lives. They were refined for the time and their place in it. More likely to become registered voters, successful black men were perceived age a threat to the status quo. Wells decided to do investigative research. She scavenged old court records and newspapers from the late 1800s and pioneered investigative journalism.

After three months, she uncovered the trends of economic and political gains in the records of the young, black men being accused of white rape and lynched. Her research also disclosed information about consenting, loving relationships between white women and black men. Wells wrote about these items and published her findings in her paper.

Her article was picked up and reprinted on the front page of a Memphis city newspaper. In an editorial response, the Memphis paper praised the patience of the Southern whites and literally put a price on Wells's head stating that "any ... black scoundrel [being] allowed to live and utter such loathsome and repulsive calumnies ... would not be tolerated."

Wells was in Philadelphia when this editorial calling for her murder was printed. Her newspaper office was looted and burned by whites. She was advised not to return. Her response was another editorial that provided names, dates, places, and circumstances documenting the hundreds of lynchings that supported her story.

Her story was the seed for what was to become the international campaign against lynching. She tried to influence the NAACP's men of power to take a visible stand against lynching. However, they didn't, and she withdrew her membership. She ultimately made her home in Chicago.

Sources:

Lynne Olson, *Freedom's Daughters: The Unsung Heroines of the Civil Rights Movement from 1830 to 1970.*

National Women's History Museum, *Women with a Deadline,* https://www.nwhm.org/online-exhibits/.

June 2008

Chapter Twelve
On Her Wash

~

*A*merican educator Catharine Beecher, sister to Harriet Beecher Stowe, promoted women's education and was an early advocate of dignifying housework. She identified laundry as "the American housekeeper's hardest problem." Women rarely could stray far from their wash. Their education opportunities were all but washed away.

Absent of running water, gas, or electricity, hand-laundry took astronomical amounts of time and labor. Gallons of water for each wash had to be transported from pump or well or faucet to stove and tub, in buckets or wash boilers that might weigh fifty pounds. Women lugged these and then heavy baskets of wet laundry outside; hung each item on the clothesline; and, later, took down each item. Women ironed by heating several irons on a stove, alternating them when they cooled, as dirty dishes stacked and waited. Regardless of social or economic status, women sought relief.

In the mid-nineteenth century, machines to alleviate the endless work of washing clothes and dishes were being designed by men and women. The scrub board appeared in 1797, displacing the rock and a hard place. Manual clothes washing machines appeared in 1846, and a rotary washing machine was patented in 1858. By 1875, over two thousand patents had been issued in the United States for various washing devices. Not every patented invention worked.

Margaret Plunkett Colvin (1828–94) of Battle Creek, Michigan, patented her invention of a rotary washing machine that did work very well. When presented at the Philadelphia Centennial, her Triumph Rotary Washer was deemed to be the "successful result of years of experiment by a practical woman." It was also presented at the World's Colombian Exposition in Chicago in 1893.

Ellen Eglin of Washington, DC, did not patent her 1880 clothes wringer invention. Rather, she sold it to an agent for eighteen dollars in 1888. She reasoned that, were it known that a Negro woman had patented the invention white ladies would not buy her wringer.

A wooden machine, with a hand-turned wheel that splashed water over dishes was patented by a man in 1850 as the first dishwasher. It wet but did not truly "wash" the dishes.

Josephine Garis Cochran (1839–1913) of Shelbyville, Illinois, daughter of an engineer, and intolerant of servants breaking her fine china, wanted a dishwasher in her own home. Dismayed at the lack of progress developing such a product, Cochran declared in disgust, "If nobody else is going to invent a dishwashing machine, I'll do it myself." And she did.

Her design featured a wire crate constructed to hold dinner plates, cups, and saucers that fitted into a wheel that lay flat in a copper boiler. From the bottom of the boiler, a motor pumped up hot, soapy water (truly "washing" the dishes) followed by a clear, hot water rinse, while the wheel containing the dishes spun in rotation. Cochran patented her dishwasher in 1866 and introduced it at the World's Colombian Exposition in Chicago. At the expo, her machine won an award for "the best mechanical construction for durability and adaptation to its line of work." It was the expo's top invention entry.

Having recognized its product potential, Cochran founded the Crescent Washing Machine Company in the 1880s to manufacture and market her mechanical dishwashing machine. Crescent built both hand- and power-operated dishwashers. Cochran anticipated the public would welcome her invention. However, since her machine was large and used an abundance of hot water, only hotels and restaurants could consider it because the hot water heaters in most homes could not supply ample hot water. Decades later, however, advancements in other home appliances opened the home market for dishwashers.

In the early 1900s, the Hobart Manufacturing Company had begun producing the first electrically driven machines for grinding food items, such as coffee beans, peanuts, and hamburger. In 1915, Hobart acquired Troy Metal Products and introduced the first model of an electric mixer designed to mix large quantities quickly. In 1924, Hobart's Troy Metals subsidiary was renamed the Kitchen Aid Manufacturing Company with headquarters in Dayton, Ohio. Two years later, Hobart acquired another appliance manufacturer that would figure prominently in Kitchen Aid's future, the Crescent Washing Machine Company.

With the acquisition of the Crescent Company, more than forty years after Cochran had presented her design, Hobart, already recognized as a leader in the commercial dishwasher market, began to further explore the feasibility of producing a dishwashing machine for use in the home.

Research and development curtailed during World War II but resumed in the late 1940s. And, in 1949, Hobart introduced to the public a new home dishwasher, the KD-10. It featured a patented washing mechanism, the Kitchen Aid brand name, and Cochran's design as the first home dishwasher. In the 1950s, dishwashers became a product popular with the general public. The Kitchen Aid home dishwasher soon established a reputation for reliability.

Josephine Cochran was honorably inducted in the National Inventors Hall of Fame in 2006. The National Inventors Hall of Fame has honorable inducted 402 inventors of which, 13 are women and 389 are men.

Sources:

EnchantedLearning.com, "Women Inventors, http://www.enchanted learning.com/inventors/women.shtml.

Robert Osborn, "Women and Washing Dishes: Two Lessons," *WaterCrunch* http://watercrunch.com/2010/08/women-and-wash ing-dishes-two-lessons/.

Autumn Stanley, *Mothers and Daughters of Invention: Notes for a Revised History of Technology*, (Scarecrow Press, Inc., 1993).

April 2009

Chapter Thirteen
She Saw in Circles

*I*n the east, west, north, and south, all saw better thanks to Tabitha Babbitt, who invented the circular saw in the early 1800s. Babbitt, a Shaker, was an early American toolmaker and inventor. While working in her and her husband's sawmill, she noticed the wasted energy of the push forward effort, with cutting accomplished only on the back pull.

Kate Braid, carpenter and poet, poetically recorded this history in the following work:

Woman's Touch

Lunchtime, sitting on a lumber pile
in the middle of the construction site,
my eye fell
on Sam's 32 ounce hammer
with the 24 inch handle.

'How come all our tools
are longer than they are wide?'
I asked.

Silence.

Feeling reckless
with confidence because that morning I'd cut
my first set of stairs
at a perfect fit, I pushed on.

'How come the hammer,
the saw, the everything
except the tool belt looks like
you know what?'

'Don't be so sensitive.' Sam said.
'How else could they be?'
There was a chorus of grunts
in the bass mode.
'Besides,'
Sam was on firm ground now,
'the circular saw is round.'

Ed raised his head slowly.
'The circular saw was invented by a woman,'
he said, and took a bite of salami.
He finished the meat and then sat
quite still, contemplating his Oreo.
'In 1810 in New England,' he continued.
'Sarah Babbitt's husband had a sawmill
where they cut logs over a pit
with a man at each end of a huge hand saw.
She noticed they wasted half
their energy, for hand saws only cut
on the push. She had an idea.'

Ed took a chocolate bite and chewed.
Even Sam was quiet.
'She went into her kitchen,
fetched a tin dish and cut
teeth in it. Then she slipped it
onto the spindle of her spinning wheel,
fed a cedar shake into it
and the circular saw was born.'

Ed folded his brown paper bag.
After a certain silence
Sam spat.
'I knew there was something funny
about that saw', he said
and sulked off stomping sawdust.

Credit:

Kate Braid, *Rough Ground Revisited* (BC: Caitlin Press, 2015), www.
    katebraid.com.

Source:

Kate Braid, *Ms.* Magazine, 1992.
January 2006

Chapter Fourteen
Olympic Women a French Start
~

Records of the ancient Olympics date from 776 BC until they were banned toward the end of the fourth century AD. During that entire period, women were completely excluded. Pausanis wrote, "Virgins were not refused admissions as spectators," but married women were not admitted on pain of death. Women were also barred completely from the first modern-day Olympics, held in Athens in 1896.

Four years later, in 1900, nineteen women—allowed to compete in golf, tennis, and yachting—made their Olympic debut in France at the games that were part of the Paris World's Fair. Female athletes were accepted as long as they remained "ladylike."

The 1920 Olympic Games saw more women competing in more events, but female competitors continued to face restrictions and reprimands. US figure skater Theresa Weld was scolded for including a salchow (jump) in her program. Women competed in tennis, swimming, and diving, but track-and-field events were still considered masculine sports, dangerous to the feminine nature, and better left to men with strength and speed.

Five track-and-field events for women were added in the 1928 Olympics, but tennis had been barred and would not be reinstated until 1988. This was also the first year of the Winter Games, in which the only competition open to women was figure skating.

The first American Olympic Games, held in LA in 1932, included the first Olympic Village. The village was for men only. No new sports for women debuted that year, but two track-and-field events were added. Louise Stokes and Tidye Pickett, two African American women, qualified but were not allowed to participate. Babe Didrikson was one of 127 women allowed to compete. In three hours, she won five events, tied a sixth, and chalked up two world records. The press called it, "the most amazing series of performances ever accomplished by an individual, male or female, in track and field history."

The 1936 Games in Berlin added gymnastics as the new sport for women. And Tidye Pickett was allowed to participate, as was another track-and-field athlete, Jesse Owens.

Wilma Rudolph earned a place on the 1956 US Women's Olympic team in Melbourne and won a bronze medal. *Time* magazine wrote of Rudolph, "She was the fastest woman the world had ever seen." In 1960, Rudolph was the first American woman to win a gold medal (she actually won three) since 1936, when Elizabeth Robinson, of Riverdale, Illinois, won the first female track gold medal. African American, Rudolph became an American icon embraced by people of all races the world over. In her speech, she pledged to use her physical talents to the "glory of God, the best interests of my nation, and the honor of womanhood."

Women dominated the 1998 Olympics in Japan, winning four of the six US gold medals. Team USA won the first ever Olympic gold medal in women's hockey. This culminated a hundred-year struggle to gain recognition and respect for women's hockey—and, in many ways, all female athletes—in North America, where the sport was often viewed with a wink as sportscasters and rink-side pundits would say, "not bad, for the girls." But the networks suffered the worst Olympics ratings in thirty years. Anheuser-Busch felt programming ignored male viewers. A spokesman said, "You have to make sure women are intrigued with the Olympics. But we're now concerned that the pendulum is so far over that the 21- to-34-year old male is saying that 'you're not talking to me anymore.'"

In 2002, more than three thousand women competed in a growing number of sports. As role models to the millions of women watching, they demonstrated that being "ladylike" was no longer the only definition of a woman.

This year, in 2004, women will have their own competitions in every sport category but boxing. Female wrestling will debut. And men and women will compete against each other in sailing and equestrian events, as they have for many years. The US women's basketball team is expected to dominate as the historic Olympic Games return to Athens with Grace and Glory and Dawn and Diana and Lisa and Tina and Sheryl and Shannon and Tamika and Sue and Swin and Yolanda and Katie and Ruth and …

Sources:

Jan Leder, *Grace & Glory: A Century of Women in the Olympics.*

Lissa Smith, ed., *Nike is a Goddess: The History of Women in Sports, Chicago Tribune,* February 24, 1998.

National Geographic, August 2004.

August 2004

Chapter Fifteen
Kevlar, Cookies, and Cocktails

~

Sometime during a holiday of your choice, raise a glass in celebration of women, three mentioned here, who paid their toll that we might more safely explore space and more.

In the 1940s, socialite Margarita Sames served a drink made with tequila, fresh lime juice, and Cointreau to guests in her Acapulco home. They called it the Margarita. Indigenous Mexicans have long known the medicinal value of tequila. *Abuelas* splash it on grandchildren's cuts and bruises. A tequila massage is said to increase relaxation while also detoxifying the skin. As the analgesic qualities of tequila soak into the skin and tissues, its aroma helps you relax.

Ruth Wakefield's restaurant in a converted Toll House Inn was once a rest stop for horses to grab some hay or oats on journeys from Boston to New Bedford. As co-owner, manager, hostess, and cook, Ruth kept very busy. One hurried day in 1930, without time to melt chocolate and pour it into the batter, she simply broke the chocolate into chunks and tossed them into the mix, thinking they would melt. After baking, she stared at her pan of "ruined" cookies speckled with chunks of chocolate. But the cookies remained ruined only until they had been tasted. A sudden jump in sales of chocolate bars in the eastern region caused Nestlé to investigate this lady. They bought the rights to her recipe, which is printed on the back of each chocolate chip package. Many cooks are creative with variations of chocolate chip cookies; some even add oats.

Kevlar, a material once a mere fiction in Superman's suit, is now a fact. As a research chemist for DuPont, Stephanie Kwolek developed a crystalline solution she wanted spun into fiber. But a technician refused to spin it, stating the solid particles in the material would clog the tiny holes of the spinneret. Stephanie knew solid material was not in her solution and, over the course of weeks, persuaded the technician to spin it. The results were astonishing. In 1971, she had invented a remarkable technology and a fiber that would forever change the field of polymer chemistry and make many millions of dollars for DuPont. This amazing material improves the performance of snow skis and is found also in boats, bullet-resistant vests, athletic shoes, boots, airplanes, and more. It is strong yet can shave eight hundred pounds off an aircraft frame. NASA used a twelve-mile Kevlar cable (thinner than a pencil) to secure a 1,200-pound satellite during a space shuttle mission. It can be used whenever and wherever a very strong, stiff, lightweight fiber is needed. Any ideas? Enjoy your holiday!

Sources:
    Catherine Thimmesh, *Girls Think of Everything.*
    S. Bertrand, *Chicago Tribune*, October 17, 2004.
    Ms., Summer 2004.
December 2004

Chapter Sixteen
St. Louie Women

～

*J*ulia Cerre (1775–1845) was born to one of the wealthiest families to settle in early St. Louis. Her father, prominent merchant Gabriel Cerre, owned large tracts of land.

In France, Antoine Pierre Soulard, escaped the guillotine in the French Revolution, sailed to America, and settled in St. Louis in 1795. Antoine married Julia that same year and received sixty-four acres of land from his new father-in law. He was appointed surveyor general of the entire province of Upper Louisiana, acquired a great deal of land himself, and resigned after several months of tending to his fruit orchard.

Julia Cerre Soulard was a philanthropist who donated considerable tracts of land to the city and to various charities during her marriage. However, after the Louisiana Purchase in 1803, ownership of the sixty-four-acre Soulard farm was mired in legalities. Eleven years after Antoine's death in 1825, Julia finally secured rights to the land. She bequeathed two blocks to the city upon her death, on condition it would remain "in perpetuity" a market as begun in 1779, when farmers would bring their wagons, form a circle, and sell their wares. Soulard Market was and is the city's primary farmers market, now it is a major St. Louis tourist attraction as well.

Charlotte Stearns Eliot, also an early settler of St. Louis, was born in 1843 of early New England family heritage. She was the daughter-in-law of Washington University founder William Greenleaf Eliot. Albeit a brilliant scholar in high school, she was unable to attend college because of her gender. Being barred from full use of her intellect did not restrain her. As a social reform activist during the era of social reform championed by

Jane Addams, Eliot was known as the "mother" of the St. Louis juvenile court system.

Through her poetry and writings, addressed the need for women to be part of the cultural and political life of their country, she openly opposed women's restrictive sphere. Her article "The Higher Education of Women" advocated for women to have's access to the male confines of higher education. It was written in the era in which Marion Talbot founded the American Association of University Women (AAUW) in 1881.

Author of several published books, articles, and poems Eliot's literary excellence was not to be recognized for many years hence. To her seventh and last child, T. S. (S for Stearns), Charlotte Stearns Eliot was his first awareness of a writer seriously engaged in writing poetry. His poetic talent has been attributed to her genes, and during his adult years of writing, he always kept her aware of his "works in progress."

Josephine Baker was born in the slums of St. Louis in 1906. As a child, she scavenged for food in garbage cans and danced for coins on street corners, where she slept beneath cardboard coverings. There, too, she experienced the 1917 race riots in East St. Louis. At age fifteen she joined a vaudeville show and left St. Louis to appear in an all-black musical, *Shuffle Along*. Four years later, she traveled to Paris as the lead dancer in *La Revue Negre* and went on to become a world famous performer and exotic dancer. By 1927, she was the highest paid entertainer in Europe. Her fame and fortune abroad, however, did not eradicate the racism she encountered when home in America.

Baker expatriated to Paris, became a French citizen, and served with the Free French Army as an informant and ambulance driver during World War II. Many of her songs sung over the radio carried coded messages to the Résistance. She was awarded France's highest military decoration the gold *Croix de Guerre* (which she melted down to help fund the war effort). She also received the Rosette de la Résistance and was made a chevalier of the *Légion d'honneur* by General Charles de Gaulle.

Baker had a lifelong dream that people of all creeds and colors would live in harmony. In her adopted country, she married and adopted fourteen children of different nationalities. She bought a country chateau she called, Village du Monde (world village) and left performing to devote her time to this, her most valued venture. But with finances failing and her husband having fled, she returned to performing in 1959.

When in the United States, Baker continued her challenge to racism. She refused to perform in clubs or theaters that segregated. Thus, she integrated many establishments, especially in Las Vegas. A prominent activist in the civil rights movement, Baker worked with the NAACP. She was the only woman invited to speak at the 1963 March on Washington, DC, next to Martin Luther King, Jr.

After King's assassination in 1968, Coretta Scott King asked Baker to replace her husband as leader of the American civil rights movement. After much consideration Baker declined, citing her commitment to her adopted children.

Sadly, in 1975, her life and her lifelong dream ended. Her property had been foreclosed upon, she was bankrupt, and she suffered a cerebral hemorrhage home alone in her own bed, where she was found in a coma four days later.

An icon in France, she received a state funeral in Paris, with full French military honors, attended by thousands. Poor at death, just as she was as a child in St. Louis when she scavenged for food behind Soulard Market, Josephine Baker would later be inducted into the St. Louis Walk of Fame and Hall of Famous Missourians.

Sources:

Cassandra Laity and Nancy K. Gish, *Gender, Desire, and Sexuality in T.S. Eliot.*

http://lcweb2.loc.gov/diglib/legacies/loc.afc.afc-legacies.200003212/
http://www.findagrave.com/cgi-bin/fg.cgi?page=gr&GRid=88163689
http://www.stlouiswalkoffame.org/inductees/josephine-baker.html
http://www.house.mo.gov/famous.aspx?fm=4
http://en.wikipedia.org/wiki/Josephine_Baker.

June 2009

Chapter Seventeen
The Oldest Profession-al Women
~

*P*rostitution as recorded in Genisis is found in the biblical narrative of Tamar, a young, childless widow. Because she was a woman, Tamar could not inherit her husband's property but remained tied to his family and was expected to have sexual relations with his brother, Onan, that she might produce a male heir. Refusing to split his inheritance with a male born to Tamar, Onan spilled his seed on the ground rather than impregnate Tamar. Like his brother, Onan died young. And Tamar remained a childless widow, economically impoverished.

In a society that valued women for their childbearing abilities, Tamar had no value, was considered worthless, and was discarded by her father-in-law, Judah. Realizing she has been abandoned and was destined for economic despair, she set in motion a plan to secure her financial future.

Pursuing the only wage-earning work available to biblical women who needed to provide for themselves, prostitution, Tamar disguised herself and sat in the roadway to await a patron seeking to buy sexual intercourse. Tamar was propositioned by none other than Judah. He offers her a sheep as payment for his purchase of sexual intercourse. She accepted and wisely asked for his seal, cord, and staff. He complied.

When it became known that Tamar (still bound to Judah's family though not integrated in it) was pregnant, her act of sexual intercourse was openly revealed as one of promiscuity and trespass against Judah's dignity. Judah's initial reaction was to have her burned. However, when his seal, cord, and staff—evidence that he had impregnated her with his child—were revealed, he immediately reconsidered. He affirmed Tamar's worth and welcomed her back into his household. In so doing, he could claim her unclaimed inheritance, her labor, and her.

Tamar gained economic stability because the man who engaged in prostitution with her thinking she was a whore, also had the power to exonerate her from scorn as well as the power to honor her upon discovering he had impregnated his daughter-in-law, not a whore, as he had intended.

Prostitution, constructed and imbued with moral gender interpretations, has plagued and provoked societies since Genesis. Globally, in the United States, Canada, Thailand, England, France, and Queensland in Australia, everything necessary to work as a prostitute is illegal, although it is not illegal to be a prostitute. Rather than to legalize prostitution as work, thereby regulating it through business codes, most governments place it under police-controlled state regulations.

Charles Winick, professor of sociology at the City University of New York, and Paul M. Kinsie, a renowned expert on the study of prostitution, wrote, "Our social structure is threatened by people who engage in sexual activity for pay." Simultaneously, our social structure legally protects sales of sexual and sensual literature, art, films, and lyrics; pornography and gender jokes and jesting; and on and on—by virtue of the First Amendment right to free speech and the Fifth Amendment due process clause of the US Constitution.

In the business of sex sales that are legally protected, the seller who profits often is successful, gains status, independence, and is described as a publisher, director, manager, executive, and so forth, titles positively associated with entrepreneurs, mostly men. While simultaneously, in the business of sex sales that are legally regulated, the seller often does not profit, often is arrested, often looses status, sometimes independence, is not described as a professional, but usually as a whore and/or its derivatives, slut, hooker, harlot, and more, words negatively associated with sex sales, are mostly women.

Many prostitutes explain the law as an institutionalized attempt to isolate and silence women. Canadian author Susan G. Cole describes prostitution as "an institution of male supremacy." In Pompeii, prostitution was a respected, recognized, and taxed women's business venture.

Be it legal or illegal, moral or immoral, prostitution is a business of supply and demand. Business, as usual, has long been a man's world, with no women allowed, except perhaps as prostitutes doing business outside the law in the oldest profession, as the oldest professionals.

Sources:
Charles Winick and Paul M. Kinsie, *The Lively Commerce*.
Gail Pheterson, *A Vindication of the Rights of Whores*.
Sarah B. Pomeroy, *Goddesses, Whores, Wives, and Slaves*.
Christine Overall, "What's Wrong with Prostitution? Evaluating Sex Work," *Signs* (University of Chicago Press, Summer 1992, 708).
May 2007

Harriet Russell Strong – Dam/Irrigation Engineer
Courtesy of the Whittier Historical Society

Jennie Pettway and other girl with quilter Jorena Petway
Courtesy LOC

Maggie Lena Walker – American Bank Founder
Courtesy of the National Park Service

Ethel Payne – First Lady of the Black Press
Courtesy Library of Congress
Public Domain

Mary White Ovington – NAACP Founder
Courtesy Library of Congress – Public Domain

Attny. Belva Ann Bennett Lockwood – U.S. Presidential Candidate
Special Collections Research Center, Estelle and Melvin Gelman Library,
George Washington University, Washington, D. C.

Unita Blackwell – Mississippi Mayor 1976-2001
Courtesy of William Patrick Butler Photography
williampatrickbutler.net

Attny. Mary Ann Shadd Cary – Newspaper Publisher
Public Domain

Josephine Garis Cochran - Dishwasher
Inventor 1893 Chicago Exposition
Public Domain

Wilma Rudolph -Track & Field Athlete/Olympic Gold Medals Winner
Corbis Image

Stephanie Kwolek, Chemist/Kevlar Inventor
Courtesy of the Hagley Museum and Library

Josephine Baker – Dancer/Civil Rights Activist
Courtesy Library of Congress
Prints and Photographs Division Washington, D.C.

Julia Ward Howe – Created Mother's Day for Peace
Public Domain

Normandy Beaches Lct R Wac Nurses
Courtesy of J Williams Colchester, Essex UK

Nettie M. Stevens, PhD - Chromosomal Geneticist
Courtesy of Special Collections Bryn Mawr College

Sarah Josepha Hale –Publisher/Editor of
Female Improvement Magazines
Portrait by James Reid Lambdin 1831
Public Domain

Huda Shaarawi - 1920s Egyptian
Feminist Union President
Courtesy Public Domain

ENIAC Women: Ruth Lichterman (left) & Marlyn Wescoff (right)
Programming First Software Hand Calculations into First Computer
Courtesy U.S. Army Photo
Public Domain

Sybil Ludington – Warned Colonists of British
Attacks in Revolutionary War
USGOV/Public Domain

Molly Williams - First U.S Female Firefighter/Former Slave
thehistoryreader.com
Public Domain

Chapter Eighteen
Mother's Day
⁓

The first North American Mother's Day was not at all the celebration we know today. It began as an antiwar day, a Mother's Day for Peace, and it began with one woman. The wars were the US Civil War and the Franco-Prussian War. The woman was Julia Ward Howe.

During the Civil War, Howe penned the famous "Battle Hymn of the Republic," an incredible theological call to arms. In it, she uses arousing Christian images to sanctify dying and killing for a cause—in this case, to end slavery. Her words reflect Christian doctrine to sing out, "As he died to make men holy, let us die to make men free." Similar holy, but non-Christian doctrine would one day be considered a jihad call to terror in future and far distant wars.

But in 1870, after reading of the Franco-Prussian War that had devastated much of Europe, Howe had an epiphany. an insight into the reality of dying and killing for just causes; especially as it pertained to sons of mothers, it occurred to her that, on the battlefield, sons of mothers, killing sons of other mothers, all sons dying in the practice of war. It awakened a consciousness in her that all those dying were sons of mothers. She not only pondered why nations did this to one another, but also asked herself what women might do to spoil the spoils of war. Howe asked, "Why do not the mothers of mankind interfere in these matters to prevent the waste of that human life of which they alone bear and know the cost?"

She appealed on a global scale—to all women of the world, particularly those who had sent a son to war. Having written the hymn twelve years earlier, Howe now wrote her Mother's Day Proclamation speaking to women worldwide of their sacred right as mothers to protect human life.

She implored women the world over to awake to the knowledge of the sacred right vested in them as mothers to protect human life.

> She wrote:
> Our husbands shall not come to us reeking with carnage, for caresses and applause. Our sons shall not be taken from us to unlearn all that we have been able to teach them of charity, mercy and patience. We, women of one country, will be too tender of those of another country to allow our sons to be trained to injure theirs. From the bosom of a devastated Earth a voice goes up with our own. It says: 'Disarm, Disarm!' In the name of womanhood and humanity, I earnestly ask that a general congress of women without limit of nationality, may be appointed and held at someplace deemed most convenient, to promote the alliance of the different nationalities, the amicable settlement of international questions, the great and general interests of peace.

Howe traveled to London in 1872 to initiate a Women's Peace Congress and began observing Mother's Day as a day devoted to the advocacy of peace doctrines. She was able to personally funded celebrations for twelve years, but without her financial support, Mother's Day for Peace had no support, and celebrations ceased.

A women's group in West Virginia led by Anna Reeves Jarvis was organized to celebrate an adaptation of Howe's holiday. It was a Mother's Friendship Day designed to reunite families and neighbors divided between the Union and Confederate sides of the Civil War. After Anna Reeves Jarvis died in 1905, her daughter Anna M. Jarvis politically campaigned for the creation of an official Mother's Day in remembrance of her mother and in honor of peace.

On May 10, 1908, her first Mother's Day celebration took place at Andrew's Methodist Church in Grafton, West Virginia, where her mother had spent over twenty years teaching Sunday school. By the next year, forty-six states, as well as parts of Canada and Mexico, were holding Mother's Day services.

Anna M. Jarvis devoted herself to the creation of a Mother's Day. She petitioned state governments, business leaders, women groups, and others. In 1914, President Woodrow Wilson signed Mother's Day into national observance on the second Sunday in May. But it became a holiday exploited extraordinaire. Its commercialization greatly disturbed Jarvis, and she vociferously opposed what she perceived as a misuse of the holiday.

In 1923, she sued to stop a Mother's Day event, and in the 1930's she was arrested for "disturbing the peace" (no less) as she protested the sale of Mother's Day flowers being sold by an American War Mothers group. She also petitioned against a postage stamp featuring her mother, a vase of white carnations, and the words *Mother's Day*. The words were removed but not the flowers. When Jarvis fought to copyright Mother's Day in 1938, it was too late to stop the commercialization.

Despite her opposition to the flower industry's perceived exploitation of the holiday, flower sales on Mother's Day continued to grow. *Florists' Review* wrote, "Miss Jarvis was completely squelched." Still, some mothers who lost a child to war continue to observe the day as a protest against war. Modern-day Mother's Day is a $15 billion industry.

Anna Jarvis died blind, poor, and childless. At the time of her death in 1948, over forty countries throughout the world observed Mother's Day. The Florist's Exchange, anonymously and unbeknownst to Anna, had paid for her extended care. Perhaps the group did so in appreciation of their good fortune, thanks to her. Or perhaps they even did it in thanks and appreciation for her—for her work, for her mother, and for her Mother's Day.

Sources:

http://www.mothersdaycentral.com/about-mothersday/history/

Valarie Ziegler, "Julia Ward Howe: The Woman Behind Mother's Day," *Democracy NOW!* "War and Peace Report," May 6, 2005

April Vitello, "Mother's Day Celebration Reaches 100th Anniversary," *USA Today*, May 10, 2008.

May 2010

Chapter Nineteen
Bewitched, Battered, and Bewildered

A history of domestic violence:

- **753 BC, Rome**. Wife beating is accepted and condoned. Laws permit the husband to beat his wife with a rod or switch, as long as its circumference is no greater than the man's right thumb—hence, "the rule of thumb." The tradition of these laws is perpetuated in English common law and throughout most of Europe.

- **AD 300**. Church fathers reestablish the husband's patriarchal values and authority of Roman and Jewish law. Constantine the Great has his wife burned alive when she is no longer of use to him.

- **900–1300 (Middle Ages)**. European noblemen beat their wives as regularly as they beat their serfs; male peasants follow their lords' example. The Church sanctions the subjection of women. Priests advise abused wives to win their husbands' good will through increased devotion and obedience. A medieval theological manual gives man permission to "castigate his wife and beat her for correction …"

- **1400s**. The Christian church supports wife beating while encouraging husbands to be more compassionate and use moderation in punishments of their wives. A Christian scholar writes Rules of Marriage. It supported wife beating.

- Law in early America follows English common law, which permits wife beating for correctional purposes. Husbands are allowed to whip their wives with a switch no bigger than their thumb.

- **1500s, England**. Women and children are taught it is their sacred duty to obey the man of the house. Violence against wives is encouraged throughout this time.

- **1792**. *A Vindication of the Rights of Women* by Mary Wollstonecraft seeks changes in this education for women and kinder treatment by husbands and lovers.

- **1861**. John Stuart Mill writes *The Subjection of Women*. He waits eight years to publish the essay, thinking the public was not yet ready to accept his argument for equality between the sexes.

- **1866**. The American Society for the Prevention of Cruelty to Animals is formed. It predates the Society for the Prevention of Cruelty to Children (1875). Both predate any organization preventing cruelty to women.

- **1871**. Alabama is the first state to rescind the legal right of men to beat their wives. Massachusetts followed by declaring wife beating illegal that same year.

- **1882**. Maryland passes the first law that made wife beating a crime.

- **1924**. A French court rules that a husband does not have the right to beat his wife. Before that, the Napoleonic Code ruled. It suggested, "Women, like walnut trees, should be beaten every day."

- **1966**. A Chicago study reveals that, from September 1965 to March 1966, 46.1 percent of major crimes perpetrated against women took place in the home. By this time, every state except Hawaii has passed child abuse report laws.

- **1967**. The state of Maine opens one of the first women's shelters in the United States.

- **1970**. In Chicago and many US cities, married battered women who left their husbands are denied welfare due to them based on their husbands' income.

- **1971**. In Kansas City, Missouri, 40 percent% of all homicides are of spouse killing. In almost 50 percent of the cases, police had been summoned five or more times within a two-year period before the homicide.

- **1972**. In Kansas City, Missouri, domestic disturbance calls were 82 percent of the total calls for that year. In Detroit, 4,600 battered women's cases "disappeared" as they moved through the criminal justice system. Only 300 went to trial.
- ***Ms.* July 1972**. Magazine reports on a bowling alley ad in Michigan. It reads, "Have some fun. Beat your wife tonight. Then celebrate with some good food and drink with your friends."
- **1974**. Boston City Hospital reports that 70 percent of ER assault victims are women attacked in homes by husbands or lovers.
- **1974**. Fairfax County, Virginia, one of the wealthiest counties in America, police reported 4,073 family disturbance calls; and that approximately 30 assault warrants were sought each week. Cites domestic violence is not just a ghetto issue.
- A *Time* article on Erin Prizzey's Chiswick Center appears only in the European edition, suggesting spousal battering was not of interest in America.
- **1975**. The National Organization for Women declares marital violence a major issue and establishes a National Task Force on Battered Women/Household Violence.
- **1976**. The Domestic Violence Act is established in the United States.
- **1978**. The House, by a vote of 205 to 201, fails to pass the Domestic Violence Act of 1978. The Senate passes it.
- **1981**. The Office on Domestic Violence is dismantled after President Reagan's election. By November, the National Center on Child Abuse and Neglect could site no federally funded programs for battered women.
- **1989**. The Brooklyn Supreme Court sentences a Chinese immigrant to five years probation for using a claw hammer to smash the skull of his wife. Citing traditional Chinese values about adultery and loss of manhood, the court ruled he was driven to kill his wife. The court stated that, due two extenuating circumstances, he was as much a victim as was his wife. The decision sent a message to

battered immigrant women that they had no recourse against domestic violence.

- **1992**. US Surgeon General ranks abuse by husbands as the leading cause of injuries to women aged fifteen to forty-four. And the FBI reports that 1,431 women were killed by their husbands or boyfriends.
- **1994**. Congress passes the Violence Against Women Act, creating, for the first time, a federal right to sue an assailant for gender-based violence.
- **2000s**. Across America, though differing by states, domestic violence is not a crime in and of itself. Attached to any underlying crime, it can be a felony or a misdemeanor: Or it can be dismissed.

Source:

Minnesota Center Against Violence and Abuse, http://www.mincava. umn.edu;

http://www2.uvawise.edu/pww8y/Supplement/ConceptsSup/Gender/ HerstoryDomV.html

March 2009

Chapter Twenty
Abortion Anthology

❧

*A*bortion was practiced in ancient Greece and in the Roman Era. Greek and Roman law afforded little protection to the unborn. In America, abortion prior to quickening was considered perfectly legal and acceptable prior to 1800. Abortion was viewed with less disfavor in 1787 when the US Constitution was written than it is currently.

By the 1840s, abortion had become a common, commercialized practice in most states. The use of both abortion and contraception remained widespread throughout most of the nineteenth century. Newspapers advertised pills, midwives' services to women, and the availability of "novel inventions" to assist women who did not want children for health or financial reasons. A woman enjoyed a substantially broad right to terminate a pregnancy. Most jurisdictions followed English common law rule that abortion with a woman's consent and prior to quickening was not a crime.

Between 1840 and 1860, a number of antiabortion laws were enacted, but these generally "preserved" the woman's right to end her pregnancy prior to quickening. Law in all but a few states until the mid-nineteenth century, was lenient with abortion before quickening.

In the early nineteenth century, the birth rate among whites began to fall. A rise in abortion, particularly among "respectable" married women, played an important role in this demographic. A doctors' crusade initiated in the 1850s led to the enactment of "restrictive" abortion legislation in the next several decades. The campaign, organized by male doctors, focused on moral and safety concerns, as well as on white, native-born Protestants' fear of being outbred by Catholic immigrants. The White Anglo-Saxon

Protestant (WASP) elite of the Northeast became increasingly aware of their small-family pattern, as opposed to the large-family pattern of immigrants and the rural poor. Eugenicists advocated selective use of contraception and sterilization to ensure the survival of the "superior stock."

Widespread sterilization became possible in America at the end of the nineteenth century with the perfection of safe and simple operations for both sexes. Compulsory sterilization laws had a markedly gender bias. The sterilization of criminals was directed at men. There is evidence that courts were reluctant to order men sterilized. Sterilization of women, however, was deemed crucial to ending feeblemindedness; of those sterilized for that reason, two-thirds were women.

In Buck v. Bell (1927), the Supreme Court upheld the compulsory sterilization of the feebleminded. The famous decision of Justice Oliver Wendell Holmes declared, "Three generations of imbeciles are enough."

But in *Carrie Buck's Daughter*, biologist Stephen Jay Gould illustrated a subtle gender bias in sterilization abuse when he wrote of how there was no evidence that Carrie Buck, her mother, or her daughter were deficient mentally but that Carrie Buck, one of several illegitimate children, was institutionalized to hide the pregnancy that had resulted from her rape by one of her foster relatives. Not only was Carrie Buck blamed for her pregnancy, but also, as Gould's article suggested, her improper sexual behavior was considered a key indicator of feeblemindedness.

In the middle and late nineteenth century, the quickening distinction disappeared from the law. Abortion before quickening was made a crime in Connecticut in 1860. After the Civil War, antiabortionists persuaded states to toughen their laws, and by 1910, every state except Kentucky had made abortion a felony.

Constitutional protection for procreation dates from the 1942 Supreme Court decision in Skinner v. Oklahoma. The case dealt with compulsory sterilization of certain felons on equal protection grounds. The decision in Skinner invalidated a state statute authorizing sterilization of persons convicted two or more times of felonies "involving moral turpitude." Skinner used heightened scrutiny, asserting that the statute, which only authorized sterilization of embezzlers and certain other criminals (mostly men), violated the Equal Protection Clause on the ground that it "forever deprived [them] of a basic liberty."

In Skinner, Justice William Douglas explained, "We are dealing here with legislation which involves one of the basic civil rights of *man*. Marriage and procreation are fundamental to the very existence and survival of the race. The power to sterilize, if exercised, may have subtle, far-reaching and devastating effects. In evil or reckless hands, it can cause races of types which are inimical to the dominate group to wither and disappear. There is no redemption for the individual whom the law touches. Any experiment that the State conducts is to his irreparable injury. He is forever deprived of a basic liberty." The protection it accorded procreation as "fundamental to the very existence and survival of the race" reflected a rather sharp break with the view held of sterilization and reproductive rights earlier in our history.

By the 1950s, a large majority of jurisdictions banned abortion however and whenever performed, unless to save or preserve the life of the mother. It has been argued (1) that these laws were the product of a Victorian social concern to discourage illicit sexual conduct and (2) that they reflected concern with abortion as a medical procedure—when most criminal abortion laws were first enacted, the procedure was a hazardous one for women—and were designed to "protect" pregnant women. In other words, the laws were to restrain women from submitting to a procedure that placed their lives in serious jeopardy. Modern medical techniques have altered this. Consequently, any interest of the state in protecting the woman has largely disappeared. The state has a legitimate interest in seeing to it that abortion, like any other medical procedure, is performed under circumstances that ensure maximum safety for the patient. Some say the state, has a duty to protect prenatal life.

By the 1960s, fourteen states had liberalized abortion laws. Roe v. Wade (1973) elevated the issue to the national political agenda. The legal reforms leading to Roe v. Wade were little more than a return to the legal status of abortions a century earlier.

Barbara Joan Zeitz, M.A.

Sources:

David M. O'Brien, *Constitutional Law and Politics.*

Ralph J. Lindgren & Nadine Taub, *The Law of Sex Discrimination*, 2nd ed.

February 2006

Chapter Twenty-One
With Woman
❧

*A*ncient Jews called her wise woman. In France, she is *sage femme*; in Germany, *weise frau* or *Hebamme*, mother's adviser, helper, or friend; *cum mater* in Latin; and *comadre* in Spanish and Portuguese. All mean 'with woman,' as does the English translation, midwife.

In ancient Greece and Rome, birth was usually an all-female event. It affirmed women's status in the patriarchal family, and midwives were held in high esteem. Their knowledge and skill in birthing assisted and celebrated the normalcy of birth.

During the sixteenth and seventeenth centuries, male midwives and medical practitioners showed interest in the procedures of women's labor and birthing. They stimulated obstetrical innovation and established private obstetrics courses—for men. By the end of the eighteenth century, male practitioners assisted in 50 percent of deliveries in parts of England, France, and the United States. This new group of physicians who called themselves obstetricians instituted protocols for hospital birth that became routine in the United States. They called for the abolition of midwifery and home birth in favor of obstetrics in a hospital.

In 1915, Dr. Joseph DeLee, author of the most important obstetric textbook of that period, defined birth as a destructive pathology, not as a normal function. In the first issue of the *American Journal of Obstetrics and Gynecology* (written and published by men), he proposed "interventions" designed to save women from the "evils natural to labor." He was head of obstetrics at Northwestern University and chairman of obstetrics and gynecology at the University of Chicago. Barring any scientific rationale, he changed the culture of women's labor and delivery in the United States.

Women, excluded from medical training, were effectively excluded from assisting with new childbirth methods in hospitals that employed the new techniques, instruments, and obstetrical knowledge. Pregnant women became convinced they were safer in the hands of doctors and hospitals, and elite, urban women began to prefer male physicians. By 1935, midwives attended only 12.5 percent of all births.

Midwives who continued to serve poor, mostly black women, came to be portrayed as dirty and illiterate. Physicians labeled them as incompetent and ignorant, in spite of studies that contradicted these charges. Lack of organization, political power, and economic resources made it extremely difficult for American midwives to defend themselves against the growing medical profession. Birthing had evolved from a physiological event into a medical procedure. And by the 1960s, most American women were unaware of any other way to give birth.

National policies also shaped midwifery. It was declared illegal in most jurisdictions, and by law, women were not permitted to use medical instruments. But as the obstetrical revolution gathered momentum, the maternal mortality rate increased. The increase was attributed to lax antiseptic practices and poorly trained birth attendants. The risk of dying in childbirth in 1863 and 1934 were virtually identical. In the Netherlands, where one of every three births occurs at home, the 1992 infant mortality rate was the tenth lowest in the world. The United States was ranked twenty-second.

In Europe, where citizens have national health care service, midwives normally perform prenatal care. In many wealthy, industrialized countries with national health care services, expensive and unnecessary health care interventions tend to be avoided to minimize unnecessary procedures and costs. In countries where health care is a business, not a service, there is less incentive to avoid expensive and unnecessary interventions, as more health care interventions provided can provide more business for private doctors and hospitals.

The "nurse-midwife" first appeared in America in 1925, with Frontier Nursing Service (FNS) founded by Mary Breckinridge, a World War I public health nurse for the Red Cross in France. The nurse-midwives' role began to broaden in the 1960s and 1970s. In 1982, the Midwives' Alliance of North America (MANA) was founded partly to focus on the midwifery model of birth care, not the medical model of birth care.

In the 1990s, US policy makers considered employing nurse-midwives as a potential low-cost solution aimed at lowering the nation's high infant mortality rate. The rate, in part, was linked to the inability of many poor, high-risk pregnant women to pay for obstetrical care and to the fact that, because they couldn't afford care, they didn't seek it. Policy, however, was not legislated.

Studies document cost savings and safe births when care is provided by nurse-midwifery. Midwives, when asked what they do that makes this so, believe the answer lies in their name. They are "with woman."

Sources:

http://nacpm.org/about-nacpm/history/.

http://www.faqs.org/childhood/Me-Pa/Obstetrics-and-Midwifery.html.

http://www.encyclopedia.com/doc/1G2-3402800303.html.

December 2009

Chapter Twenty-Two
Ladies D-Day
⁓

*I*t was not just one day. It was many days, many months, and many years of strategy to end a war of many nations. The day beginning the end of that war, the Allied invasion at Normandy on June 6, 1944, would become known as D-Day.

Addressing the soldiers, sailors, and airmen of the Allied Expeditionary Force before the invasion, General Dwight David Eisenhower said, "You are about to embark upon the Great Crusade, toward which we have striven these many months. The eyes of the world are upon you. The hopes and prayers of liberty-loving people everywhere march with you." But it is not noted that Eisenhower's remarks also included that the eyes of the world were upon, or if the hopes and prayers of liberty-loving people were with the female nurses who served their country alongside the male soldiers, sailors, and airmen to whom Eisenhower directed his remarks.

During World War II, Congress authorized that women could serve in auxiliary forces to assist the armed services. Hundreds of thousands of American women joined military programs that would accept them—the Women's Army Auxiliary Corps and women's divisions of the Navy, Air Force, Coast Guard, and Marines. More than fifty-nine thousand women served in the Army Nurse Corps, many in makeshift hospitals on or close to the front lines.

The Army Reorganization Act provided that nurses receive a "relative" temporary rank of second lieutenant to major. "Relative" rank gave women army nurses the right to wear the military insignia but without the military status of privileges. For example, nurses did not rate the salute, a sign of military respect, and nurses, it was deemed, did not need or receive full military training. As well, the female nurses received half the pay of equally ranked male officers.

No one kept records of these fifty-nine thousand nurses, not the military, not even the US Veterans Administration. Women military nurses after the war were not allowed membership in veteran groups. Schoolbooks did not mention them or their service. All forms of media all but overlooked them; none of those whom the nurses helped to liberate and keep free asked about their military service. Unable to answer questions not posed, they did not speak. The nurses, unnoticed, stood silent.

Lt. Frances L. Nash, RN, was one of the nurses deployed to a military hospital in Manila in 1940 as the United States prepared for the possibility of war. After the attack on Pearl Harbor and the Philippines, General Douglas MacArthur ordered troop withdrawal to the Bataan Peninsula. Nash recalled being told the nurses were to remain until all staff members and supplies had been evacuated and to prepare to be taken prisoner. Nash was, in fact, captured, along with sixty-six other army nurses who had remained behind with her. Once captured, they worked as nurses in the prison camps for the next three years, until the war ended.

During the first Allied amphibious invasion at North Africa on November 8, 1942, Lt. Helen Molony was one of fifty-seven army nurses with meager military combat training serving with the inadequately equipped and staffed Forty-Eighth Surgical Hospital. The unit landed with the combat troops to serve in the dangers of a combat zone. Dressed in full battle gear, helmets, and field packs, they could have been mistaken as male soldiers, save for the rifles issued to the combat troops but not to the nurses.

Well before the invasion, the Red Cross was preparing for the club mobile program's move to the continent. The exact date the army took the Red Cross into their confidence regarding the D-Day invasion is not known, but it was probably in spring 1943.

When Andrea Noto and her brother were growing up, she never heard her mother talk about her wartime activities. Occasionally, when a program on TV would show scenes from World War II, her mother would start to cry and say, "What you see on television is just a coating of what it was really like."

Anna Donato, RN, graduated in 1941 from Greenville Hospital School of Nursing in Jersey City, New Jersey, and in 1943, enlisted in the United States Army. She decided to enlist before she was drafted. The Bolton Act was signed in 1943 to draft nurses into military service. It was never necessary to draft a nurse.

Lt. Donato's military service took her to the beaches of Normandy for the D-Day invasion. Donato recalled being one of only three nurses chosen for a secret mission to land with the troops that day. The army has never confirmed this, stipulating only that this information has not been declassified.

Eileen O'Connell Byrne was a Chicago public school nurse from the 1960s through the 1980s. What her school children never knew—they didn't ask, and Byrne didn't tell—was that, during the 1940s, she was an army nurse who served during the D-Day invasion.

Byrne's oldest daughter, Isabelle, wrote to me, "My mother was very proud that she had been part of U.S. Armada and had come down the rope ladder off a troop ship just like all who were there on D-Day. She was with the troops under General Omar Bradley."

Eileen O'Connell grew up on Chicago's West Side, graduated from St. Joseph Nursing School in 1935, and worked in psychiatric hospitals with some of the most violent patients until 1940 when she volunteered to serve as an army nurse after the United States entered the war.

Security regulations meant she couldn't tell her father where she was training. She saw active duty when she traveled by landing barge from England to Utah Beach, one of the five sites of the D-day invasion, to care for the wounded soldiers, both Allied Forces and POWs alike. Observing a German soldier with severe burns being ignored by an American doctor, she pulled rank and took over his medical care stating, "I don't care who you are. I'm a first lieutenant."

In 1948, Eileen married Charles Byrne, who died young. She was widowed at age forty-eight with five children. She went back to school and earned her bachelor's of science in nursing and, in 1962, became a public school teacher-nurse. She actively promoted and was part of the training film that introduced the Head Start Program in the 1960s.

For some fifteen of her twenty-two years with the district, Byrne also worked nights in a nursing home for financial reasons. Her daughter Eileen, Jr., noted her mother never slept during this time, only taking catnaps as she could. After her mandatory retirement at age seventy, Eileen worked at a day care center, until called back by the Chicago schools as a nursing consultant, where she worked until she was ninety-two. And when the board of education budget was tight, she volunteered to serve the schools, as she had once volunteered to serve the nation on Ladies D-Day.

National Nurses Week is celebrated in May every year!

Suggested video:

 Canteens & Lipstick: WWII Nurse Recalls Invasion of Normandy on D-day (see details below)

Sources:

 Helen Rameriz-Odell, *Working Without Uniforms.*

 Evelyn M. Monahan and Rosemary Neidel-Greenlee, *And If I Perish.*

 http://www.cps.edu/Spotlight/Pages/Spotlight317.aspx.

 http://www.defense.gov/news/newsarticle.aspx?id=26360.

 http://www.kens5.com/story/news/local/heroes/2014/06/06/canteens-and-lipstick-wwii-nurse-recalls-invasion-of-normandy-d-day/10616046/.

 http://www.qaranc.co.uk/d-day-normandy-landings..php.

 http://www.redcross.org/news/article/Red-Cross-Retrospective-Workers-Land-on-Normandy-Beach-1944.

June 2012

Chapter Twenty-Three
Dos Equis

~

*S*ince ancient times, it had been believed that the sex of an infant was determined by the degree of heat a man's sperm had during insemination. Aristotle claimed that the male principle determined sex in the fetus and if the male principle was "insufficient" during reproduction, the fetus would develop as a female.

More than two thousand years of scientific speculation and experiments on how an animal, plant, or human becomes male or female followed. No one had discovered the chromosomal basis of sex determination as to why a female, why male or why certain diseases struck either males or females but not both. Then in 1905, a woman told the world why; actually, she told the world X and Y.

Geneticist Nettie Marie Stevens, PhD, presented her chromosomal research on sex determination in a scientific paper titled, "Studies in Spermatogenesis with Especial Reference to the 'Accessory Chromosome.'" It was a Carnegie Institute Report.

The report documented her findings, which established that the sex of basically all many-celled biological organisms is determined at the moment of fertilization by the combination of two kinds of microscopic entities—the large X and the smaller Y chromosomes—and that these two chromosomes, responsible for determining the sex of individuals, depended specifically on the presence or absence of the smaller Y chromosome.

Her findings ended a long-standing scientific debate as to whether sex was determined by heredity or other factors. It influenced the entire field of genetics and opened doors for research in science and medicine that continues to this day. It was one of the major twentieth-century scientific breakthroughs.

Stevens was born July 7, 1861, in Cavendish, Vermont, to a middle-class family that had lived in New England for five generations. She grew up in Westford, Vermont, during the post–Civil War years when few opportunities other than teaching, nursing, and secretarial work were available and acceptable for women who wanted a profession rather than a man. Nettie wanted to be a scientist and wanted an education.

But even higher education for women was limited and frowned upon. Women who wished to pursue higher education were discouraged and often criticized. Choosing to attend the colleges and universities that accepted women rather than choosing marriage could be daunting for a woman. But Stevens's father, a carpenter and handyman, did well enough and could afford to send his children to school at the Westford Academy, which accepted men and women.

Stevens was a brilliant student with a penchant for science and mathematics and consistently scored the highest in her classes. She graduated from Westford at age nineteen and hungered to further her education. But with middle-class economics challenging her higher education expenses, Stevens became a teacher so that she could work to earn and to save money to attend college.

After three terms, she had saved enough to attend the Westfield Normal School, a teachers college, now Westfield State University, in Massachusetts. Stevens completed the four-year course in two years, graduating at the top of her class.

Her pattern of working, saving, and returning to school was to repeat itself. During her next break from furthering her education, she taught for ten years before earning enough to further her education

Then, in 1896 at age thirty-five, she traveled west across an early American frontier to attend Stanford University in California. At Stanford, she earned her bachelor of arts in 1899 and her master's of arts in biology in 1900 while working at the Hopkins Seaside Laboratory. Her thesis involving precise, microscopic detailing of new species of marine life would become a factor in her success with later investigations of chromosomal behavior.

Stevens continued to work her way through college to once again return to graduate school, this time back east at Bryn Mawr College for Women in Philadelphia, the first college to offer PhDs to women. There she earned her doctorate in 1903. She was made a research fellow funded by the Carnegie Institute, and she was awarded a fellowship to study abroad.

She traveled to Europe to study in Theodor Boveri's lab at the Zoological Institute at Würzburg, Germany, where Boveri was working on the problem of the role of chromosomes in heredity. Likely, her interest in the subject developed during this fellowship.

Afterward, Stevens began to look for a research position and was given an assistantship by the Carnegie Institute, thanks to "glowing" recommendations from Bryn Mawr biology professor Thomas Hunt Morgan; biology department chair Edmund Wilson; and M. Carey Thomas, president of Bryn Mawr. Wilson, a close friend of Boveri, went on to join the zoology department at Columbia University and invited his good friend Morgan to join the Columbia staff as professor of experimental zoology.

Stevens, now age thirty-nine, finally was able to begin working as a research scientist through the Carnegie fellowship, and the next eleven years would be the most productive of her life. But the fellowship meant she still had to teach. She wanted a pure research position and wrote to director Charles Davenport to see if it was possible for her to work at his Station for Experimental Biology at Cold Spring Harbor Laboratory. A research professorship was created for her at Bryn Mawr to work with Davenport.

Her discovery paper, when published in 1905, was not without controversy. The chromosomal theory of inheritance was not accepted by many scientists. It was staunchly believed that gender was determined by the mother and/or environmental factors. Most scientists working on sex determination did not embrace Stevens's research immediately, a common practice in early genetic discoveries, especially with regard to discoveries by women.

Wilson made a very similar discovery around the same time and submitted his paper ten days prior to Stevens. Despite having read her manuscript, Wilson's paper hypothesized that, in certain cases, females have one more chromosome than males and dismissed Stevens's data that females have two large sex chromosomes, a major fact not noticed by Wilson, who only performed tests on the testis.

Wilson eventually reissued his original paper and credited Stevens for this finding. He combined his idea of idiochromosomes with her theory of heterosomes in his future work. Simultaneous discovery is common in science, and for Wilson to decidedly cite a competitor, especially a woman, is formidable, since her findings were generally considered to have made a larger theoretical leap and were ultimately proven correct.

Morgan also published a paper arguing that specific hereditary traits could not be carried on a single chromosome. Morgan later changed his mind and surmised that chromosomes are responsible for identifiable hereditary traits. Most biology textbooks credit Morgan for mapping the first gene locations onto chromosomes of fruit flies that had become Morgan's lifetime work.

But what often is not mentioned in textbooks is that it was Stevens who introduced fruit fly chromosomal studies to Morgan in his lab in the first place. Notwithstanding, his work is considered to have formed the modern-day understanding of heredity.

Although Stevens, Morgan, and Wilson researched in proximity, in actuality, most of Stevens's work was carried out in isolation from the men, also common practice for women in scientific research at the time. Stevens's position in the field of genetics has largely been overlooked. Credit for the discovery of X and Y chromosomes and their role in determining gender is generally given to Wilson and to Morgan, who together shared the 1933 Nobel Prize in physiology for the discovery.

Stevens, who published thirty-eight papers in eleven years, was awarded the Ellen Richards Research Prize (given to promote scientific research by women). She continued to do research and teach at Bryn Mawr and Cold Spring Harbor Laboratory for the rest of her life but was unable to occupy the professorship created for her, as her life ended much too soon after a brilliant career that had started much too late.

Dr. Stevens's life was taken by breast cancer when she was just fifty-one, on May 4, 1912. Still, in one decade, this scientist possessing two Xs of her own contributed more to genetics than scientists possessing one small y of their own and having much longer careers. Notably, she left it to posterity to research and determine how her discovery of the large X and the smaller Y chromosomes that defined sex determination relegated her another noble but not Nobel scientific woman. Y? Dos Equis?

Sources:

http://www.dnaftb.org/9/bio.html;   http://en.wikipedia.org/wiki/
Nettie_Stevens.

http://www.nature.com/scitable/topicpage/nettie-stevens-a-%20
discoverer-of-sex-chromosomes-6580266.

May 2012

Chapter Twenty-Four
Mag Women

~

T he first magazines published in the American colonies—there were two—appeared in 1741. These and subsequent early magazines were founded by men and directed to male readership. Articles focused on social life, politics, and women. The articles about women primarily debated women's roles in and out of the home, connecting to these roles notions of loyalty, morality, family, politics, and the new nation.

Women's magazines surfaced in the post-Revolutionary period and were primarily literary. The first, *Lady's Magazine and Repository of Entertaining Knowledge*, founded in Philadelphia in 1792, contained no information on women and household work, fashion, or beauty. The magazine's most notable feature was a tribute to Mary Wollstonecraft's *Vindication of the Rights of Women*, also first published in 1792.

Still, the topics of household work, fashion, beauty, and fiction came to define women's magazines in the more than forty publications that appeared by 1830. Unlike men's magazines, women's magazines paid little attention to current events or nonfiction. Nonetheless, these early women's magazines provided an important outlet for women writers and editors and paved the way for future publications aimed at women.

The emergence and public presence of women writers and the new debates they engendered was evidenced in Nathaniel Hawthorne's infamous remark about the "damned mob of scribbling women" writers for these publications. And although many of the early women's magazines were short-lived, their failures must be put in context, recognizing that men decided family spending and which magazines were purchased - or not. Subsequently, however, circulation rates of women's magazines grew as advertising began to finance production costs.

Godey's Lady's Book was the most successful monthly magazine directed to female readership. Founded in 1830 in Philadelphia by Louis Antoine Godey and edited by Sara Josepha Hale from 1836 until 1877, *Godey's* was dedicated to "female improvement." Articles did not focus on household work but primarily on women's education. It ceased publication in 1898 but had laid a solid foundation for future women's magazines. Hale is often credited for making Thanksgiving a national holiday in the United States and is the author of a collection, *Poems for Our Children*, one of which is "Mary Had a Little Lamb."

Mary Louise Booth founded and was editor of *Harper's Bazaar* from its beginning in 1867 until her death in 1889. Booth was a prolific translator; she translated into English the works of French authors and her *Harper's Bazaar* was America's first fashion magazine. It began as a weekly publication catering to women in the middle and upper classes. It showcased fashion from Germany and Paris in a newspaper-design format. In 1901, *Harper's* became a monthly publication. William Randolph Hearst, who formed the Hearst Corporation in 1887, purchased the magazine in 1912.

Ladies' Home Journal began in 1883 as a single-page supplement titled *Women at Home* written by Louisa Knapp Curtis in a farm magazine published by her husband. A year later, it became its own independent publication—*Ladies' Home Journal and Practical Housekeeper*—with Knapp as editor. Knapp, who dropped the last three words in 1886, published the work of muckrakers and social reformers such as Jane Addams. Within ten years *LHJ* became the leading magazine of its type, with a circulation of more than one million, and was known as the "monthly Bible of the American home."

Fundamentally, women's magazines continued the pattern of addressing white, married women in the home, be they middle class or upper class. Magazine publications aimed at diverse women did not emerge until the 1960s, with *Cosmopolitan* as one of the most notable. *Cosmopolitan* was first published in 1886 as a family magazine that transformed into a literary magazine. Revamped by editor Helen Gurley Brown in 1965, it became a women's magazine that catered to the single woman.

The *Advocate* started in 1967 as a weekly publication aimed at gay and then lesbian audiences. *Essence*, the first mass magazine aimed at African American women, was founded in 1968 by Denise M. Clark and others. Essence Communications Inc. (ECI) began publishing in May 1970, with a circulation of approximately fifty thousand copies per month.

Ms. Magazine, founded by Gloria Steinem, began as a one-page insert in *New York* magazine in 1971 and as its own issue in 1972. *Ms.* responded to and helped popularize the women's liberation movement by publishing articles about politics, child care, women's health, lesbian issues, and violence against women.

The magazine *Working Woman*, founded in 1976, appealed to women in the workplace, featuring financial and career issues. *Latina* magazine was founded in 1996 by Christy Haubegger, then a twenty-eight-year-old Stanford Law School graduate, frustrated by a lack of Hispanic role models in the popular media who appealed to Hispanic American women like herself.

Lear's magazine was first published in 1988 and targeted "older women." Its slogan was "For The Woman Who Wasn't Born Yesterday." It covered celebrity interviews, women's issues, and progressive issues and had next to no fashion coverage. Advertisers were want to identify the readership to target, thus *Lear's* was want for advertiser funds. Despite a circulation of 503,000, *Lear's* was forced to close in 1994, 202 years after the first women's magazine sans household or fashion articles was published in 1792.

Sources:

http://iwp.library.cornell.edu/i/iwp/women_intro.html.

Wikipedia for each magazine.

http://self.gutenberg.org/articles/essence_(magazine).

January 2011

Chapter Twenty-Five
Veiled Egyptian Protesters
~

*I*n the early 1900s, Egyptian women clad in veils defied harem convention and poured out into the streets to demonstrate with the men, as all classes rose up in protest to achieve national liberation and individual independence. And the women were gathered for yet a third cause—liberation from gender repression by Egyptian men and Egyptian mores, well before the second wave of the women's movement of the sixties.

The first demonstration broke out in Cairo on March 9, 1919, after the end of World War I. At the time Egypt was under British imperialist oppression. The protesters had been denied a meeting to discuss political demands, and Egyptians took to the streets in significant display to protest against the protectorate and martial law (imposed by the British in 1914).

Men and women protesters were strongly united, and as word about Cairo spread, more demonstrations took place throughout all of Egypt. This national uprising of both genders brought men to a moment of revisiting and relaxing their participation in the conventional harem ways in which both men and women had been raised.

The women were in the streets participating in unprecedented activities. Notably, the men needed their help. Through this national movement, men and women, husbands and wives who previously had shared separate existences of divided harem convention in their own homes and personal lives, actually were brought together. One such couple was Huda Shaarawi and her husband.

Huda wrote in her memoirs, "My husband kept me informed of events so that I could fill the vacuum if he were imprisoned or exiled." It was during this period of protests that active feminism was brought to the forefront by Huda, who'd previously had to conduct her activism secluded from public, political involvement. When the protesters formed the Wafd Party to help define their agenda, their leader, Saad Zaghlul, was immediately arrested. And after some protesters had been shot in the streets, Huda wrote her first public letter of protest.

The letter was to Lady Brunyate, an American by birth and wife of Sir William Brunyate, judicial and financial adviser to the Egyptian government. It referred to conversations the two women had previously had, during which Huda had been assured the British had taken part in World War I to "do service to the cause of justice and humanity, to protect the freedom of oppressed peoples and safeguard their rights."

Her letter was never answered, but the next month, Saad Zaghlul was released from detention and the Wafd was allowed to travel abroad for negotiations. The day after Zaghlul's release, Huda and women representing all different classes were a huge part of a peaceful and hope-filled demonstration. But at the negotiations, the Wafd was pressured by the British government to force Egyptian Prime Minister Rushdi Pasha to issue a return to order.

Huda, well acquainted with Prime Minister Pasha and supported by her women followers, wrote to Pasha asking him to resign. The British issued to him a final ultimatum to carry out orders. Rushdi Pasha resigned.

Near the end of 1919, over a thousand Egyptian women from all classes met and formed the first female political body, the Wafdist Women's Central Committee, with Huda as its president. The WWCC intent was to support the male Wafd, still in its first year of existence. But old gender-disparate customs proved hard to break.

A year later, near the end of 1920, when Wafd male leaders returned from London negotiations with a proposal of terms for independence, the proposal was shown to male groups and organizations but not to the WWCC. The women eventually did review the proposal, found the terms to be inadequate, and reported their findings to the press.

Huda sent a letter from the WWCC to Saad Zaghlul denouncing Wafd's treatment of the women who had supported the men of the Wafd. She specifically wrote that half the Egyptians, the female half, should not be denied their full rights, especially their right to participate in their nation's liberation. Zaghlul responded with a letter of apology. But gender parity within the Wafd was strained.

Near the end of the next year, Zaghlul was deported. The WWCC, led by Huda, protested his deportation in a letter to the British High Commissioner, stating this would not silence the protests, as millions of others would continue to speak out against injustice. The women became more militant. Their meetings were banned, but ironically, these feminist women were able to meet in the privacy of the harem social order. And they did.

Under Islamic law, women inherited money and property in their own name with rights of ownership. The WWCC organized an economic boycott against the purchase of British goods and advocated the withdrawal of money from British banks. They campaigned for the purchase of Egyptian goods and the deposit of their money in the new Egyptian bank, Bank Misr.

The British eventually issued a declaration of Egyptian independence that would maintain British troops stationed in Egypt and keep Egypt's political future under British authority. The new constitution cited all Egyptians equal before the law but granted suffrage to men only.

On March 9, 1923, on the fourth anniversary of the first demonstration when veiled women had first protested in the streets, Huda, with some of the same women, formed the Egyptian Feminist Union. Huda was elected president. In May, upon her return from an international feminist meeting in Rome and before a crowd of women awaiting her at the Cairo station, Huda Shaarawi stepped out onto the running board of the train and removed her veil. This act signaled the beginning of the end of the harem social system in Egypt. But obsolescent gender inequity is not yet obsolete.

Source:

Huda Shaarawi, *Harem Years: The Memoirs of an Egyptian Feminist (1879–1924)*.

March 2011

Chapter Twenty-Six
Her Kabuki/Not His
~

K abuki of today might well be defined as dance theater that features male dancers in traditional Japanese costume and makeup, performing both the male and female roles. But wait, not so fast. Women from Manchuria, China, and Korea to Japan and the Ryukyu Islands played an important role in the history of Kabuki. Women were priests, soothsayers, magicians, prophets, and shamans in the folk religion, and they were the chief performers in organized Shintoism. In Japan, these women were called *miko*.

Miko traditions date back to ancient Japanese women prophets who went into trances and conveyed the words of the gods, comparable to the Pythia or Sibyl in Ancient Greece. Toudaiki historical data tells of a woman Kuni, also called Izumo no Okuni (Okuni from Izumo), who came to Kyo (now Kyoto) dressed in a strange-looking man's costume and danced what was called "Kabuki-odori." And thus, Izumo no Okuni, a miko at the Grand Shrine of Izumo, is chronicled as the originator of Kabuki theater.

Okuni (ca. 1572–?) grew up in the vicinity of the Izumo shrine, where her father, Nakamura Sanemon, worked as a blacksmith and where several other family members served. Eventually, Okuni joined as a miko and became known for her skill in dancing and acting, as well as for her beauty. As it was custom of the time to send priests, miko, and others to solicit contributions for the shrine, she was sent to Kyoto to perform sacred dances and songs.

And so it was that, around 1603, Okuni began performing a new style of dancing, singing, and acting on the dry riverbed of the Kamo River and at Kitano Shrine in Kyoto. At a time when Kyoto was in disarray after the Battle of Shekigahara, the performances of Okuni dressed in flamboyant men's costumes delighted and caught the imagination of the people and received tremendous acclaim

Okuni's Kabuki was the first dramatic entertainment of any importance that was designed for the tastes of the common people in Japan. Early performances, often considered gaudy and cacophonous, were equally lauded as colorful and beautiful. She assembled around her a troupe of wandering female performers who danced and acted.

In order to form her troupe, Okuni accepted as her performers the female outcasts and misfits of the region, particularly those involved in prostitution, giving them direction; teaching them to act, dance, and sing; and offering them rehabilitation. Due to their eccentricity and social daring, Okuni's troupe's performances were labeled Kabuki. The word *Kabuki*, derived from the late sixteenth-century colloquial verb *kabuku*, can translate to mean "eccentric, shocking, forward leaning, out of step with the accepted norm, not conforming to the social order of the time, and perhaps even a woman (women) ahead of her (their) time."

Okuni's troupe was exclusively female. Thus, she required her actors to play both male and female roles. In particular, Okuni herself was best known for her roles as samurai and Christian priests. This new style of exclusively female troupes became known by the alternate names of *shibai* or *onnakabuki* (from *onna*, the Japanese word for "woman" or "girl").

Okuni's Kabuki quickly became very popular, and many other companies of courtesans and other female performers appeared not only in Kyoto and Edo (Tokyo) but also in many Japanese prefectures. The abuki-odori performed by these women was called *onna-kabuki* (women's Kabuki). The sensuous character of the dances (and the prostitution of the actors) proved to be too disruptive for the government, which in 1629 banned women from performing

Due to the 1629 order prohibiting the performance of onna-kabuki because it was deemed to be corrupting public morals, it gradually disappeared, and Okuni herself became absent from historic records. A new concentration was directed on *wakashu-kabuki*, performed by boys too young to shave their forelocks in adult style. However, these new troupes were also deemed to corrupt public morals, and a prohibition on wakashu-kabuki was issued around 1652.

In the beginning of the Edo period, when onna-kabuki was banned as a corrupting influence on social morals and after the second prohibition was issued against young boys, the period of *yaro-kabuki*, performed by adult males with *yaro atama* (a man's head after the forelock was shaved off) began. Men took over, even playing the female roles (*onna-gata*), and the resulting theater performances developed into the Kabuki of today.

Note: In November 2002, a statue of Izumo no Okuni was erected in her honor and to commemorate four hundred years of Kabuki. It is located on Kawabata Street at the north of the Shijo Ohashi, near the shore of the Kamo River in Kyoto.

Sources:
    http://en.wikipedia.org/wiki/Izumo_no_Okuni.
    http://www2.ntj.jac.go.jp/unesco/kabuki/en/2/2_01.html.
April 2011

Chapter Twenty-Seven
Women's Software

∾

*S*ix women programmed the technology known today as "software" for the empty computing machine that men built. His hardware with her software became the world's first computer, known as ENIAC (Electronic Numerical Integrator and Computer).

The computer machine measured 8 by 3 by 100 feet; covered 1,800 square feet of floor space; weighed thirty tons; and contained about eighteen thousand vacuum tubes, seventy thousand resistors, ten thousand capacitors, six thousand manual switches, and five million soldered joints. It completed the same computations the women's "computers" did using the slide rule, differential analyzer, and electronic calculators but in a fraction of the time, after the women had transformed their computations into software.

During World War II, the US Army wanted a computing machine that could calculate artillery-firing tables to be used to deploy weapons with target accuracy. The military sponsored research beginning in 1943. At a 1946 press event, ENIAC was presented to the public. The men who had built the machine were acknowledged and lauded in newspaper headlines across the nation. The men, the machine, and the women's software program became famous, but the women did not. The women were not even introduced. Allow me to introduce them to you.

Betty Jean Jennings was born in 1924, the sixth of seven children in a Missouri farm family that valued education. She majored in math at what is now Northwest Missouri State University, often the only girl in her classes. She wanted not to teach but to see the world and have adventures. She was twenty. Her faculty adviser noticed in a 1945 math journal that the army was recruiting math graduates for a wartime project in Philadelphia. She applied, was accepted, and was told to come quickly. She got on the next train available. Her high school principal said Betty made the highest marks in math of anyone who had ever attended the school. At the Moore School of Computing in Philadelphia, she was a "computer," who hand-computed ballistics trajectories and became one of the original six ENIAC programmers (programming the enormous machine to perform the ballistics differential calculus equations the women had calculated by hand). She and fellow programmer Betty Holberton led the programming.

Betty Snyder Holberton was born in 1917 and attended Quaker primary schools. She graduated from the University of Pennsylvania with a degree in journalism, one of the few colleges at Penn open to women in 1939. The school was not her first choice, but it provided her the opportunity to take undergraduate courses in other Penn colleges not open to women. She joined the Moore School in 1942. She and Jean devised the trajectory program that controlled the operation of the ENIAC during its presentation demonstration in 1946. Holberton also developed the first sort-merge generator for UNIVAC I for Dr. Grace Murray Hopper, who, it is said, developed her ideas about compilation from Holberton. Dr. Hopper credited Betty with being the best computer programmer she had known. UNIVAC I was the first commercial computer produced in the United States.

Kathleen McNulty was born in Donegal, Ireland, in 1921 and came to America when she was three. She spoke Gaelic, attended parochial grade school in Chestnut Hill, and Hallahan Catholic Girls High School. At Hallahan, her math studies included two years of algebra, plane and solid geometry, and trigonometry. She graduated from Chestnut Hill College for Women in 1942, one of three math majors in a class of ninety-two. She studied college algebra, math history, integral calculus, spherical trigonometry, differential calculus, and partial differential equations. As a junior, she knew she did not want to teach and began scouting employment where she could use her math, only to learn that most actuarial companies did not hire women. So as a senior, she took business classes—accounting, money and banking, business law, economics, and statistics. After graduation, she noticed in the newspaper that the army was looking for women with a degree in mathematics—right there in Philadelphia. Kay contacted Frances Bilas, a fellow math major, and together they went to interview. Both were accepted as human computers and were notified to report to the Moore School, where they were introduced to a differential analyzer for the first time.

Frances Bilas Spence was born in 1922 Philadelphia, the second of five girls. She graduated from South Philadelphia High School for Girls and attended Temple University. She received a full scholarship to Chestnut Hill College in Philadelphia, where she majored in mathematics and minored in physics. She graduated in 1942 and planned to teach—that is, until McNulty told her about the army recruiting math majors. After the two women applied and were accepted, they were happy to know they would be contributing to the war effort.

Mary Wescoff Meltzer graduated in 1942 with a degree in social studies from the Secondary Education Department at Temple University in Philadelphia. Jobs were scarce. A friend told her Moore School was hiring. Her knowledge of how to run a calculator and operate an adding machine landed her a job working on program computing. She was immediately shown how to run a Marchant calculator and took classes in calculus and trigonometry.

Ruth Lichterman Teitelbaum, whose father was a Hebrew scholar, graduated from Hunter College with a bachelor of science in mathematics and was recruited to the ENIAC group as one of the original six. She was the last of the original six to leave the ENIAC because she stayed on two years to train the next generation of programmers.

The ENIAC women developed software programming that converted math analysis into electrical impulses that made sense to a machine—enabling a calculation to travel through the machine's circuitry to completion—to thus create a functioning computer. These women established the foundation for the software of today. Yet they were effectively written out of (or never written into) computer history of the time. But times change. Fifty-one years later, the ENIAC women were inducted into the Women in Technology International Hall of Fame.

Visit the WITI Hall of Fame online at http://www.witi.com/center/witimuseum/halloffame/.

Sources:

http://www.eniacprogrammers.org/.
W. Barkley Fritz, *The Women of ENIAC*.

May 2011

Chapter Twenty-Eight
Feminine Paul Revere

*S*ybil Ludington (1761–1839) was the oldest of Colonel Henry and Abigail Ludington's twelve children. Together, Henry and Abigail owned and operated a mill in Kent, New York.

During the Revolutionary War, the colonel formed the Seventh Regiment of the Dutchess County Militia, a volunteer regiment of local men who enlisted for periods of time between planting and harvesting their crops. Training took place on the Ludington's Parade Grounds, opposite their manor house.

When Sybil was sixteen, her mother expected her to be responsible and act ladylike. As the oldest child, she had numerous duties, such as making butter, soap, and candles; baking bread; mending clothes; washing dishes; spinning, knitting, weaving, and sewing; and tending to her younger siblings. In addition, she was charged with outdoor work in the fields and mill. Still, she found time to watch her father train tired farmers into soldiers, and she knew where each one lived. She wanted to be in the militia because, just as everyone else, she wanted to be free and independent and was tired of being ruled by Great Britain.

In April 1777, the Continental Army transferred its supplies to Danbury, Connecticut, where it was deemed they would be safe and require little guard. Hospital cots and tents were stored there, along with clothing and shoes and cooking utensils. Supplies included flour, beef, pork, sugar, coffee, molasses, rice, wheat, corn, and several hundred cases of wine and rum.

On April 26, a two-thousand-man British force moved into Danbury and destroyed the supplies—save for the wine and rum, which they drank—and then drunkenly began burning settlers' homes. Danbury messengers were speedily dispatched in all directions to announce the arrival of the British and news of the fires. Late that evening, a tired messenger reached Colonel Ludington, informing him the British were burning Danbury and pleading him to muster his men to come fight the British back to Long Island Sound.

The colonel had just returned from a long session of guarding the Hudson Highlands and was exhausted. It was well into the night. The messenger was also exhausted. Moreover, he was unfamiliar with the area and would be unable to locate all of the militia volunteers in their homes scattered throughout the area.

Sybil had recently received a horse for her sixteenth birthday whom she named Star. She was very familiar with the area, knew the men would believe her warning, and told her father that she would go alert the men. She mounted Star around 9:00 p.m. that rainy night and left for her now-famous ride.

It is unclear whether Sybil volunteered or whether she was asked by her father to make the ride. Some accounts indicate that an exhausted Colonel Ludington, needing to muster the men and unable to leave, planned the route Sybil would take, despite knowing the dangers for a young girl.

The woods and swamps were full of bushwackers, cowboys, and army deserters. On her ride, Sybil would need to avoid them, as well as British soldiers, British loyalists, and "Skinners"—outlaws with no allegiance to either side in the war.

At each house she reached, she warned the men, "The British are burning Danbury. The colonel is mustering the troops." And she cautioned the families be ready to abandon their homes if the enemy should come their way. Some accounts indicate that a church bell was rung in Carmel after she gave the alarm.

It was dawn when Sybil arrived back home, soaked with rain and now exhausted herself. Colonel Ludington was already mustering the men who had come. He stopped to help his daughter from her horse with a great deal of pride and a silent prayer of thanksgiving for her safe return. She had traveled forty miles, twice the distance of the famous midnight ride of Paul Revere.

Sybil was congratulated for her heroism by friends and neighbors and was later recognized by General George Washington for her service to the war. An excerpt from Colonel Ludington's memoirs reads, "There is no extravagance in comparing her ride with that of Paul Revere and its midnight message. Nor was her errand less efficient than his. By daybreak, thanks to her daring, nearly the whole regiment was mustered before her father's house at Fredericksburg, and an hour or two later was on the march for vengeance on the raiders."

A bronze statue of Sybil riding her horse that depicts the spirit and determination of the girl and the strength of the horse is located on the eastern shore of Lake Gleneida in New York state and is illuminated at night. It continues to be a beacon of freedom, strength, and the will to win. The plaque reads: "Sybil Ludington Revolutionary War Hero April 26, 1777."

Several smaller originals of the statue also exist. One is on the grounds of the Daughters of the American Revolution Headquarters in Washington, DC. A 1975 commemorative postage stamp in the "Contributors to the Cause" United States Bicentennial series honored Sybil Ludington. A fifty-kilometer footrace is held annually in her name in Carmel, New York. Its course, on hilly roads, approximates Sybil's historic ride and finishes near her statue at Lake Gleneida.

Sources:

Patricia Edwards Clyne, *Patriots in Petticoats*.
http://www.rootsweb.ancestry.com/~nyeccdar/sybil_ludington.htm.
http://en.wikipedia.org/wiki/Sybil_Ludington.
July 2011

Chapter Twenty-Nine
Fab Fem Firefighters

~

"*I*t didn't matter if you were an Olympic athlete or if you were 6' 7" tall and the strongest woman on earth—it didn't matter," said Brenda Berkman in 1982. Women were not hired for jobs as New York City firefighters. Women were not even allowed to "apply."

That year, Berkman filed a lawsuit against New York City alleging that some of the physical exam requirements, which were unnecessary for the job itself, discriminated against women. The court ruled in her favor, and the physical exam was revised to be more relevant to the job. That year, forty-seven women passed the exam, and Berkman became the first female firefighter hired in New York City. But her fight for women's equal opportunity was not over. Realistically, it just had begun.

On the job, Berkman faced years of harassment and gender abuse. "The idea that men hated me so much that they might leave me in a burning building by myself, that they drained my air tank, that they phoned death threats to my house, that they followed me around on the street and threatened me—that was scary," Berkman said.

It is recorded that the very first female firefighter in the United States was Molly Williams in 1815. Williams was a slave owned by New York merchant Benjamin Aymar, a member of the Oceanus Engine Company No. 11 in New York City. Little is known of Williams's life, but female firefighters know her heroic story.

Often dressed in a calico dress and checked apron, she fought alongside men and had their respect. It is written that, during the blizzard of 1818, when few male firefighters volunteered, Williams helped save multiple towns by repeatedly pulling the pumper engine through deep snow to fight fires. Albeit she was only a "volunteer" firefighter, Williams's dedication and endurance paved the way for other women to become paid firefighters.

Lillie Hitchcock Coit is mentioned as an early female firefighter in 1859 San Francisco, but again she was not a paid firefighter. As a little girl, Coit had been captivated by the fire department. As a teenager, she witnessed a poorly staffed crew of firefighters responding to a fire call and threw down her schoolbooks to help drag the engine to the fire up on Telegraph Hill. After that, Coit became the engine company mascot and could barely be constrained by her parents from jumping into action at the sound of every fire bell.

She would frequently ride with the Knickerbocker Engine Co. 5. Throughout her youth and adulthood, Coit was recognized as an honorary firefighter with the Knickerbocker Engine Co. 5. Later, for her enthusiasm and unwavering support, she became patroness of all San Francisco firemen (firefighters).

In the 1920s at the age of fifty, Emma Vernell became a member of Westside Hose Company 1 after her firefighter husband died in the line of duty. She was the first woman officially recognized as a firefighter by the State of New Jersey. And again, as with other women firefighters, it appears Vernell may not have been paid for her work as a firefighter.

Judith Livers Brewer is considered to be the first paid female firefighter. Livers was hired in 1974 by the Arlington County Fire Department in Arlington, Virginia. While helping her firefighter husband study for his fire science classes, Livers was motivated to become a firefighter herself. She retired in 1999 at the rank of battalion chief.

Toni McIntosh, hired by the Pittsburgh Fire Department in Pittsburgh, Pennsylvania, in June 1976, is considered to be the first African American woman to become a career firefighter. She served for more than eleven years.

The first female hired by the Indianapolis Fire Department was a black woman named Byronna Slaughter. She was sworn in on March 3, 1978. Slaughter chose to leave the department after a short career mid reports of harassment and lack of acceptance due to her gender.

Male firefighters were often crude and rude to the women. To intimidate the women, they played demeaning practical jokes and ostentatiously displayed sexual behavior—all of which conformed to traditional, unacceptable male mores that were accepted as "boys will be boys" behaviors. Some men wouldn't even talk to the women because they felt women shouldn't be there and couldn't do the job as well as the men could.

In 1980, Lauren Howard became the first Chicago female firefighter. She joined the ranks of a protected macho profession that had been traditionally preserved for primarily white Irish men passed down in families from generation to generation. Howard was the only woman in the department for six years, when twenty female firefighters were hired in Chicago in 1986.

In the 1990s, Nancy Ducey experienced gender harassment as a woman firefighter in Urbana, Illinois. When a phone call was for her, the man who answered the phone would turn on the microphone as a signal for her to come to the phone, and then he would not speak to her. She felt the men believed that she shouldn't be there because it was a man's job. Ducey went on to become an instructor at the Illinois Fire Service Institute.

As of this year, women still remain a minuscule part of the firefighting profession. Nationwide, only 10,800 women are career (paid) firefighters, making up 3.6 percent of the career firefighter population. Women comprise approximately 4 percent of the volunteer fire service of an estimated 32,000 members. And 61,000 women are career emergency medical technicians and paramedics, representing 34 percent of the EMS workforce.

Taking the Heat, a 2003 PBS graphic documentary film, poignantly details the facts surrounding Berkman and the NYC female firefighters. In celebration of Women's History Month in March 2011, the US Fire Administration recognized the contributions of all women, past and present, to the American Fire Service—each one a Fab Fem Firefighter.

Sources:

BlackAmericaWeb News, February 5, 2010.

http://www2.scholastic.com/browse/article.jsp?id=11592.

http://www.usd116.org/ums/apple/service/department/history/
women.html.

https://i-women.org/firefighters/history-of-women-in-firefighting/.

http://www.pbs.org/independentlens/takingtheheat/film.html.

August 2011

Chapter Thirty
Weather She Qualified

~

*M*eteorology for women, prior to the middle of the nineteenth century, was not an accepted or even available area of academic study, occupational training, or employment. In America, the only acceptable occupation for women (and, unmarried only) was teaching. Still, brave, hardy, intelligent women forged paths and found ways to become atmospheric scientists.

Sarah Frances Whiting (1847–1927) was tutored in mathematics and physics by her father, a New York state college professor. Upon receiving her bachelor's degree in 1865, she taught at the Brooklyn Heights Seminary for Girls, where she attended scientific lectures and visited local laboratories, when she could. In 1875, she accepted a position teaching physics at Wellesley College in Boston, and she attended the laboratory physics classes of Edward C. Pickering at MIT. Pickering's was the first undergraduate physics laboratory in the United States. Hers was the second, which she opened in 1878 at Wellesley College.

At Wellesley, Whiting introduced a course in meteorology, put together a meteorological observing station, and had her students collect data for the US Weather Bureau. In 1895, she was the first scientist, male or female, to make weather X-ray photographs in the United States. She was the first woman invited to join the New England Meteorological Society; she was a member of the American Physical Society, which had initially refused to invite women to its banquets; she was one of five women to be elected a fellow of the American Association for the Advancement of Science; and she received an honorary degree from Tufts College.

Grace Evangeline Davis (1870–1955) studied physics and meteorology under Whiting at Wellesley, where she earned her bachelor of arts and her master's of arts degrees. Davis was the associate professor of physics at Wellesley from 1899 to 1936, best known there for her popular meteorology course. Davis studied at Radcliffe, Harvard, and MIT and was a charter member of the American Meteorological Association founded in 1919.

Gladys Wrigley (1855–1974) earned a fellowship to Yale, where she became the first woman in the United States to earn a PhD in geography, for her work put forth in her dissertation, Roads and Towns of the Central Andes, published in the *Geographical Review.* Wrigley worked at the American Geographical Society and was the first editor of the organization's highly respected *Geographical Review.* She held this position for twenty-nine years until her retirement and was one of the most influential scientific editors of first half of the twentieth century. Still, she was never invited to dine with councilors of male staff members and was referred to as "Miss Wrigley," while male PhDs were addressed as "Dr." Dr. Gladys Wrigley, PhD, was also a charter member of the American Meteorological Association.

Hundreds of thousands of opportunities for women availed themselves in the 1940s, as hundreds of thousands of men were sent overseas to fight in World War II. Meteorologist positions were opened to and undertaken by qualified women. When the men returned, the women were expected to return their positions to the *returning* men who expected this.

Bernice Ackerman (1928–95) started her career during the war with the Women Accepted for Volunteer Emergency Service (WAVES). After the war, she earned a bachelor of science in meteorology, with a minor in mathematics, from the University of Chicago in 1948 and went to work for the US Weather Bureau. She went on to earn her master's of science in meteorology in 1955 and her PhD specializing in cloud physics in 1965, both also from UC. She was an associate professor of meteorology at UC from 1965 to '67 and then at Texas A&M from 1967 to '70. Then from 1970 to '72, she was an associate meteorologist in the Atmospheric Sciences Section at Argonne National Laboratory. Ackerman's credentials are numerous. She is considered one of the most important women meteorologists of the second half of the twentieth century.

Hazel Tatro (1920–74) received her meteorological training while serving in the WAVES during World War II. She earned her bachelor of science in meteorology from Florida State University on a Weather Bureau scholarship and then worked for the Weather Bureau. Tatro was the first woman to be an MIC, Meteorologist in Charge, of a US Weather Bureau office.

Beryl Bedgood Beaurepaire was a member of the Women's Auxiliary Australian Air Force (WAAAF) in the 1940s. She chose to join the WAAAF because her father was in the air force, she was interested in science, and she understood there would be openings in the meteorological section. In her interview, she was told, "Oh no, they won't allow any women into that." She joined anyway and was able to "remuster" as a meteorological assistant with two other women in a class of forty. The three women, who needed a matriculation or a university year to be accepted, were better educated than the thirty-seven men, who needed only the equivalent of intermediate (high school) education.

Beaurepaire recalls that the men were posted to the Weather Bureau but the women worked alongside public servants. As well, the women received about a quarter of the pay of the men, with no extra pay for weekend shifts, for which the men received time and a half. The women complained to the director of the WAAAF, a woman, stating they had not joined the WAAAF to be public servants. Some months later, they were reassigned to positions more respective to their weather observation talents. Still, until the mid-1970s observer positions were not fully open to any woman despite weather she qualified.

Sources:

    http://brianna.laugher.id.au/blog/tag/bureau-of-meteorology.

    http://passporttoknowledge.com/storm/who/bios/women1.htm.

September 2011

Chapter Thirty-One
Her Head in the Clouds
~

*A*s a young girl, Joanne Simpson, née Gerould, (1923–2010), was fascinated by clouds. As a young adult, she became the first woman to earn a PhD in meteorology. But not so fast. Because she was a woman, she was unable to pursue her doctoral studies or perform her meteorological research as planned.

In 1939, as a sixteen-year-old student-pilot, Joanne was required to complete a course in meteorology. She did so at the University of Chicago, and because of her interest in clouds, she also took a course in astrophysics. Simpson was instantly hooked on meteorology and inquired about other such courses. Carl-Gustaf Rossby, considered by many to be the greatest meteorologist ever, had just arrived at the university to establish an institute of meteorology.

Simpson interviewed with him and, within minutes, was in his World War II, nine-month meteorology training program. It consisted of teacher-in-training weather instruction to fifty women, who would then teach weather to aviation cadets. In her classes at both New York University and the University of Chicago, Simpson taught weather to cadets, many older than herself, all men, and she prepared weather maps.

After the war, women were expected—many were told—to return home. But Simpson returned to college with the intent to complete her master's degree and enter a PhD program.

Simpson recalled some reactions to her scholarly plans by some Chicago professors: "They told me it was totally inappropriate for a woman to be a meteorologist. You would have to work night shifts, leaving the airport in the middle of the night. You would have to fly in airplanes to do research. You'd have to do all kinds of things women can't do."

She remembered, "Every possible obstacle was put in our way, ranging from refusal of scholarships to downright hostility from the wives as well as the men." She and two other women students were told by Rossby that no woman had ever earned a PhD in meteorology and that none ever would. And, he added, if any of them did, they would never be given jobs. The year was 1945.

About two years later, after Rossby had left the department, Simpson, who had attended a lecture on aircraft observations of wind flow and cloud structure in the tropics given by Herbert Reihl (highly regarded as the father of tropical meteorology), contacted Reihl. She was intrigued by this new field of tropical meteorology. That, coupled with her interest in clouds, now cumulus clouds, led her to asked Reihl to be her adviser in this area of study. Reihl agreed. Rossby also agreed, commenting that it (clouds) was a good subject for "a little girl" to study.

No man had devoted serious scientific research to clouds or their role in weather. It was accepted that clouds were the result of weather, not a cause. Despite Rossby's demeaning gender remark and the gender abusive atmosphere in the department from the all-male faculty, Simpson began studying tropical convection clouds in relation to tropical wind systems. She completed her doctoral work and, in 1949, became the first woman to receive a PhD in meteorology.

Her first major contribution to atmospheric science was the astounding hypothesis that tropical clouds weren't just the passive result of atmospheric circulation but were, in fact, the cause.

Drs. Simpson and Reihl went on to write landmark meteorological papers. In 1958, they proposed the "hot tower hypothesis" that clouds carry undiluted warm moist air from the ocean 50,000 feet into the air. Their findings shook the skeptical meteorological community and revolutionized meteorology itself.

Meteorologists knew the eye of a hurricane was made of a ring of towering clouds but did not know how the heat engine inside this tower of clouds worked to sustain its tremendous power while traveling great distances. They lacked empirical evidence to explain hurricane structures, their energetics, and the thermodynamics of tropical weather "cumulous clouds," seemingly considered too girlie a subject to research and study. Little was known about clouds.

But the cumulonimbus clouds (hot towers) hypothesis that scientifically suggested such clouds provide the energy needed to keep circulation and the trade winds running proved to be groundbreaking data—data to be empirically verified twenty years hence. Dr. Simpson's reputed stature in meteorological scientific research was significant. She developed the first cloud model, discovered what makes hurricanes run, and revealed what drives the atmospheric currents in the tropics.

To create the first cloud model—either an analytic equation or a computer model—had long been a dream of hers. She developed such a cloud model using a slide rule to do her calculations because computers had not yet been invented. Thus, her first model was a one-dimensional depiction of a buoyant cloud plume growing vertically. Her data and her cloud model ignited a field of cloud studies that grew from 2 or 3 meteorologists to a field of about 350 within two years.

Her career in meteorology was just beginning. But one of Rossby's remarks, the one about women not being accepted to work in the field of meteorology, proved to be true. No one would hire Dr. Simpson as a meteorologist. Undaunted, she knew her meteorological work lay ahead, for her head still was in the clouds.

Sources:

    http://geogain.org/?page_id=52.
    http://www.islandnet.com/~see/weather/history/joannesimpson.html.
    http://earthobservatory.nasa.gov/IOTD/view.php?id=43027.
    http://earthobservatory.nasa.gov/Features/Simpson/simpson2.php.
October 2011

Chapter Thirty-Two
Her Eye in the Hurricane
~

*D*uring Dr. Joanne Simpson née Geould's college days at the University of Chicago, meteorology professor Carl-Gustaf Rossby's remark about women not being accepted to work in the field of meteorology would subsequently prove to have merit. No one would hire her as a meteorologist. Turned down repeatedly because of her gender, Simpson accepted a scientific teaching position at the Illinois Institute of Technology, where she went on to become an assistant professor of physics.

At the time, atmospheric air movements in the tropics were literally unknown. Tropical weather was yet to be explored, meteorological inquiries were yet to be proposed, and interest was yet to be stimulated. There was no obvious interest by any of the men to scientifically study and research clouds. Tropical storm clouds were still thought to be a symptom not a cause of weather. Dr. Simpson, however, thought otherwise. She theorized answers to tropical weather conditions, in fact, lay directly in the very tall clouds in equatorial regions.

During her summers at IIT, she became involved in a project at Woods Hole Oceanographic Institution in Massachusetts, where she conducted research analyzing tropical clouds. Her documented data demonstrated how important clouds were in driving tropical circulations, specifically in the destructive driving forces of hurricanes. She drew maps of cloud formations that revealed specific patterns now routinely seen on satellite images. As a result of this work, she obtained a full-time position at Woods Hole in 1951.

Dr. Simpson requested that the Office of Naval Research provide the Woods Hole team with an airplane outfitted with meteorological instruments. She intended to fly the plane into the tropical clouds to gather empirical measurements to validate her computations. However, the Woods Hole director said that women were not allowed on their field trips. But the Navy officer who arranged for the aircraft, Captain Max Eaton of the Office of Naval Research, simply said, "No Joanne, no airplane." Henceforth, Woods Hole dropped its gender restrictions on all research vessels. Thanks to Dr. Simpson and, in this case, Captain Eaton as well, another door for future female researchers was opened.

In her landmark paper, "On the Structure and Maintenance of the Mature Hurricane Eye," Dr. Simpson documented self-sustaining tropical convection in the cumulonimbus clouds in the eye of hurricanes that created the heat to drive the hurricane.

By 1960, Dr. Simpson was a full professor at UCLA. There, she designed and taught graduate classes and authored two books. Her work laid out how clouds behave after being seeded, which had not yet been resolved or understood. To empirically test her first computerized cloud model, Dr. Simpson flew up above the clouds to film the activity down within her clouds. In 1964, Dr. Simpson left UCLA and took a position with the National Weather Bureau, which later became the National Oceanic and Atmospheric Administration.

In 1974, Dr. Simpson became an Endowed Chair Professor in the Environmental Science Department at the University of Virginia. But because she was a woman, she was not regarded as a real professor by the all-male faculty. Her ability to work in the traditional and tolerated gender-abusive-atmosphere in which she found herself at the university, severely restricted her ability to work. She needed equal opportunity in order to conduct her serious scientific research.

Dr. Simpson took a leave from the university to work at the new Laboratory for Atmospheres at NASA's Goddard Space Flight Center. There, she was offered the head position of the Severe Storms Branch. At NASA, she found a gender-friendly environment in which to do and expand her work and something new to her. She could talk science with other *female* scientists. She recalled how, one day in the ladies' room, she encountered two other women scientists washing their hands and discussing meteorology. Never before had she been in an office where anyone but she and the secretaries used the ladies' room. Dr. Simpson remained involved with NASA until her death.

In 1986, NASA asked Dr. Simpson to lead the Tropical Rainfall Measuring Mission. TRMM was a joint space mission study team between NASA and the Japan Aerospace Exploration Agency (JAXA) for a proposed data collecting weather satellite. The satellite mission was to carry the first space-based rain radar to measure rainfall across the tropics and subtropics. TRMM met or exceeded all its goals, and the satellite has led to remarkable meteorological discoveries. It is part of NASA's Mission to Planet Earth, a long-term, coordinated research effort to study the earth as a global system. The TRMM satellite was launched in 1997 from the Tanegashima Space Center in Japan.

Dr. Simpson was the driving force behind this first satellite mission to study tropical rainfall from space. She considered her involvement in launching the satellite, still operating today, the most important accomplishment of her career.

The American Meteorological Society's highest honor, the Carl-Gustaf Rossby Research Medal, was awarded to Dr. Joanne Simpson in 1983 for her outstanding contributions to man's understanding of the atmosphere. Ironically, the medal was named for the same Rossby who had predicted she would never find work in meteorology because of her gender. Dr. Simpson recalled, "He told me that I would look both ridiculous and pathetic if I didn't really make it big after making such an unconventional spectacle of myself in my fight to become a meteorologist."

In 1989, her colleagues elected her president of the American Meteorological Society. As the first woman to hold that position, it became just one more accomplishment - just one more of so many reasons Dr. Joanne Simpson could hold her head high in the clouds with her eye in the hurricane.

Barbara Joan Zeitz, M.A.

Sources:

http://www.islandnet.com/~see/weather/history/joannesimpson.htm.

http://earthobservatory.nasa.gov/IOTD/view.php?id=43027.

http://geogain.org/?page_id=52.

November 2011

Chapter Thirty-Three
Civil War Female Surgeon

~

US Senate Bill 82, containing a provision for an Army Medal of Honor, was signed into law by president Abraham Lincoln on December 21, 1861. The medal was "to be bestowed upon such petty officers, seamen, landsmen, and Marines as shall most distinguish themselves by their gallantry and other seamanlike qualities during the present war."

The Medal of Honor is the highest military decoration awarded by the United States government. In total, 3,475 medals have been awarded to 3,456 people—3,455 men (of whom 19 were awarded the medal twice) and 1 woman.

Mary Edwards Walker was born to abolitionists Alvah and Vesta Whitcomb Walker in Oswego, New York, in 1832. She was the youngest of five daughters and would later have one younger brother. The entire family worked the family farm. Alvah, a self-taught country doctor, and Vesta, an elementary school teacher, allowed their daughters to wear clothes suited to farm labor, not women's style of the time.

Her parents believed tight-fitting women's clothing was unhealthy. This belief was zealously adopted by Mary, who, as an adult, would advocate dress reform for women in her own pursuit of women's rights. She often wore men's clothing, as women's jeans and slacks were virtually nonexistent at the time.

Both parents believed in education and equality for their son and for their daughters. The first schoolhouse in town was built on their land. Mary attended the school where her mother was a teacher, and it was her father's medical books that spurred her interest in medicine. Her parents' encouragement instilled in her confidence she could become a doctor, even though it was a time when females were not allowed formal medical training.

As a young woman, Walker entered Syracuse Medical College, the first medical school to accept women and men equally. She worked as a teacher at the same school where her mother taught in order to earn enough money to pay her way through medical school. It cost $165 and consisted of three 13-week semesters.

Walker graduated in 1855 at age twenty-one, the only woman in her class and the second American woman to earn a medical degree. The first was Dr. Elizabeth Blackwell in 1849. Dr. Mary Walker opened a medical practice but failed to attract patients.

In 1856, Dr. Walker married fellow medical student Albert Miller. She wore a man's coat and trousers at their wedding and kept her last name. The couple moved to Rome, New York. There, they began a joint medical practice that did not prosper, most likely due to the fact that folks were not yet receptive to women physicians, who were not trusted or respected at that time.

Her marriage also did not prosper. Miller proved to be unfaithful, and the couple separated after four years. Dr. Walker briefly attended Bowen Collegiate Institute in Hopkinton, Iowa, in 1860 – briefly because she was suspended after refusing to quit Bowen's all-male debating society.

Dr. Walker then set up another medical practice. Due to social growth and more women venturing into public positions, this practice proved successful. One of her ads in the *Rome Sentinel* read, "Those … who prefer the skill of a female physician … have now an excellent opportunity to make their choice." Times for women were beginning to improve thanks to social advocates such as Dr. Walker and the steps they took into places, opening spaces for women.

When the Civil War began in 1861, Dr. Walker went to Washington, DC with the intent to join the Union Army as a medical officer. Unthinkable to the men in command that a woman (in trousers no less) could perform surgery and give medical examinations, she was denied enlistment. She volunteered and received no compensation for her surgical work, most done as a field surgeon in makeshift hospitals set up near the front lines. She served under Dr. J. N. Green as his acting assistant surgeon and performed many of his duties for almost two years, although her medical credentials were often questioned.

Dr. Walker, wearing a modified version of a male officer's uniform, was captured by Confederate troops in April 1864, taken hostage, and imprisoned. She acted as a spy, and her outrage at the improper prisoner rations resulted in the addition of wheat bread and cabbage. After four months, she was released and returned to the Fifty-Second Infantry, where she continued her medical work at the Louisville female prison and an orphan's asylum in Tennessee.

In October 1864, Dr. Walker finally became commissioned as an acting assistant surgeon earning one hundred dollars a month. She was the first female surgeon commissioned in the US Army. President Andrew Johnson, acting on the recommendations of Major Generals William T. Sherman and George H. Thomas signed a bill in November 1865 that gave Dr. Walker the Congressional Medal of Honor. The citation recognized her "valuable service to the government," devoting "herself with much patriotic zeal to the sick and wounded soldiers, both in the field and hospitals, to the detriment of her own health," and enduring "hardships as a prisoner of war."

After the war, Dr. Walker became a writer and lecturer, advocating for issues such as health care, temperance, women's rights, and dress reform for women. She wrote two books that discussed women's rights and dress, and she introduced the use of the postcard. She interacted with Susan B. Anthony and Elizabeth Cady Stanton on women's suffrage and agreed with Anthony that women already had the right to vote and Congress needed only to enact enabling legislation. Anthony's words in the Nineteenth Amendment state that the "right to vote cannot be denied on account of sex," not that the right to vote can now be given to the ladies.

In 1917, the US Congress changed the criteria for the Congressional Medal of Honor, and Dr. Walker's medal was revoked. That year, her health began to decline. She refused to return the medal and wore it illegally every day until her death two years later at age eighty-six. Dr.

Walker had a plain funeral, but an American flag was draped over her casket. She was buried in her black suit instead of a dress. Her birthplace is marked with a historical marker.

Family and friends lobbied incessantly to have Dr. Walker's medal reinstated. Sixty years after it was revoked, in 1977, President Jimmy Carter signed an order doing just that—citing Dr. Walker's distinguished gallantry, self-sacrifice, patriotism, dedication, and unflinching loyalty to her country despite the apparent discrimination because of her sex.

A 1982 US postage stamp was issued in her honor, and in 2000, the Women's Hall of Fame at Seneca Falls, New York, inducted the only woman awarded the US Congressional Medal of Honor, Dr. Mary Edwards Walker, Civil War female surgeon.

Sources:
http://en.wikipedia.org/wiki/Medal_of_Honor.

http://www.bilerico.com/2011/10/dr_mary_edwards_walker
_civil_war_surgeon.php.

http://www.northnet.org/stlawrenceaauw/walker.htm.
December 2011

Chapter Thirty-Four
Her Military Time

~

- **1802**. West Point was created when President Thomas Jefferson signed legislation establishing the United States Military Academy as an institution devoted to the arts and sciences of warfare. It was in response to several soldiers and legislators, including George Washington (during his presidency), Henry Knox, Alexander Hamilton, and John Adams who had urged the establishment of such an institution to eliminate America's wartime reliance on foreign engineers and artillerists. Jefferson asserted to ensure that those attending the Academy represented a democratic society. That democratic society representation, however took another 174 years before Academy enrollment accepted female cadets. In 1976, the 4,000 Corps of Cadets included 119 women, of whom 62 graduated four years later.

- **1839**. The Virginia Military Institute was founded on the site of the Lexington state arsenal and was the last US military college to admit women. VMI is a public institution, not a private one, and taxpayers' dollars, especially women's taxpayer dollars, should never be used to discriminate against women. That said, VMI spent millions of taxpayer dollars to keep women out, arguing that accepting women cadets would destroy its methods and its mission. The 1991 Supreme Court decision that allowed women to attend the all-male VMI may be Ruth Bader Ginsburg's most famous case. Attorney Ginsburg reformulated the question before the court to be not whether a female could be admitted to the all-male VMI but whether the government could constitutionally deny admittance to a qualified applicant because of gender. The 1997 first co-ed class consisted of thirty women who were held to the same strict physical courses and technical training as the male cadets, until it became apparent that adjustments to the standards had to be made. VMI resisted following other military colleges in adopting gender-appropriate physical training standards until 2008, when it was listed as a goal in VMI's 2039 Strategic Plan.

- **1842**. The Citadel in Charleston and the Arsenal in Columbia, South Carolina, were converted into military academies by Governor John P. Richardson through an act of the state legislature. In his message to the legislature in 1842, the governor spoke eloquently of the educational purpose to be served by converting the state's arsenals to serve educational needs. Three years later, they merged into one academy, The Citadel and the Arsenal Academy. The first class graduated six male cadets. General Mark Clark, upon his retirement from the army, became president of The Citadel in 1954. Clark established The Citadel Summer Camp for boys and revitalized the college's varsity sports programs. Academic programs established in the 1960s that continued to serve the educational needs of South Carolina included the undergraduate Evening College in 1966 and Graduate School programs in 1968. But despite the governor's eloquent words of 1842, and subsequent academic improvement programs, The Citadel did not serve the needs of women until 1996, when women were first allowed admission to its Corps of Cadets. This came after two years of legal battles, when The Citadel was forced to enroll Shannon Faulkner, whose application the academy had previously accepted, having assumed Shannon was male.

- **1850**. The United States Naval Academy became a reality after a history that began during the American Revolution in 1794, when President George Washington persuaded Congress to authorize a new naval force to combat the growing menace of piracy on the high seas. In 1825, President John Quincy Adams urged Congress to establish a naval academy "for the formation of scientific and accomplished officers." His proposal, however, was not acted upon. A naval school was established in 1845 without congressional funding at a ten-acre army post called Fort Severn in Annapolis, Maryland, with a class of fifty midshipmen and seven male professors. The curriculum included mathematics and navigation, gunnery and steam, chemistry, English, natural philosophy, and French. In 1850, the naval school became the US Naval Academy. And in 1933, Congress authorized the academy to begin to award bachelor of science degrees. The academy later replaced a fixed curriculum taken by all midshipmen, no midshipwomen, to study a wide variety of elective courses and advanced study and research opportunities. Women were first allowed enrollment and access to these opportunities in 1976, though it took an act of Congress.

- **1951**. The Defense Advisory Committee on Women in the Services (DACOWITS) was established to provide advice and recommendations on matters and policies relating to the recruitment, retention, treatment, employment, integration, and well-being of highly qualified professional women in the armed forces. Composed of civilian women and men appointed by the Secretary of Defense, DACOWITS' recommendations have been very instrumental in effecting changes to laws and policies pertaining to military women.

- **1954**. The US Air Force Academy was authorized by Congress and signed into existence by President Dwight David Eisenhower. The academy, paid for with male and female taxpayer dollars, barred women cadets until 1976, after President Gerald R. Ford signed legislation put forth by Congress permitting women to enter the nation's military academies. A statement on the USAF Academy's official fact page reads, "Perhaps the most controversial event in academy history was the admission of women."

- **1998**. The issue of sexual harassment allegations and redress, or lack of it, in the military drew heavy media coverage regarding a case in Fort Belvoir, Virginia, where the credibility of six female accusers, all in military uniform, was questioned while the accused male military defendant was exonerated. Former democratic congresswoman Patricia Schroeder who specialized in military and gender issues during her tenure in the House feared the trial would reinforce women perceived as second-class citizens in the military. A statement from the dean of George Washington Law School, indicated the case, "may make women reluctant ... even fear coming forward."

- **February 2002**. A panel was created to help address the problem of sexual assault within the military. But the Pentagon let the panel's charter expire. Still known as DACOWITS, the board no longer advises the military on sexual assault.

- **February 2003**. Following decades of sexual harassment incidents reported at all military academies, a major sex scandal at USAF Academy became public. Twenty female cadets said they faced swift punishment after making formal reports, while accused male assailants went about their lives, and investigations revealed that nineteen had been commissioned as officers.

- **March 2003**. Five former board chairwomen contacted Defense Secretary Donald Rumsfeld to resist pressure to disband the board from conservative administration advisers who thought it was fostering "radical feminism" and was not needed because women had been integrated into the military.

Sources:

http://www.usma.edu/wphistory/SitePages/Home.aspx.

http://www.citadel.edu/citadel-history/brief-history.html#origins.

http://www.usafa.af.mil/information/factsheets/factsheet.asp?id=9409.

http://www.usna.edu/USNAHistory/; http://dacowits.defense.gov/.

http://www.nytimes.com/1998/03/15/us/when-character-counts.html?pagewanted=all

http://www.washingtonpost.com/archive/local/1996/01/20/vmi-has-
spent-14-million-in-battle-to-keep-women-out/0a891338-ada7-
478e-bec5-c059d9756d11/.
January 2012

Chapter Thirty-Five
Women in Black

~

*I*n 1988, twenty years after Israel occupied the West Bank and Gaza, the Palestinian intifada began. In response, Israeli Jewish women began to stand in weekly silent vigils in busy public places. They wore black. Hecklers abused them in sexual ("whores") and political ("traitors") terms. Their policy was not to shout back but to stand silent and dignified. Women in Black support vigils were soon organized in Canada, Australia, many European countries, and many US cities. In Italy, a group of women founded their own Women in Black, Donne in Nero.

In London, in 1991, women demonstrated as Women Against War in the Gulf in opposition to US-led bombardment of Iraq. Afterward, some renamed themselves Women in Black. Women in Black vigils are held weekly in Trafalgar Square, as well as in many countries and cities around the world. In Serbia, the war between the former Yugoslav Republics in 1991 gave birth to Women in Black in Belgrade, Zene u Crnom. Still active today, this group opposes aggression and masculine violence with weekly vigils in Belgrade's Republic Square. And they partner with men who refuse to serve in the military.

Women in Black are in Brussels, Femmes en Noir, and in Flemish-speaking Leuven, Vrouwen in het Zwart. Women in Black in Spain, Mujeres de Negro, are strong and active. In Tokyo, Women in Black often walk silently, single file, through shopping areas. Some visit and support women in war zones.

Women in Black in India began in 1992 when the ancient mosque Babri Masjid was torn down by Hindu fundamentalists and violence engulfed India, with women the main victims. WIB hold silent vigils on the streets, in market squares, and in Gandhi Peace Park.

In the Philippines, Women in Black began in 1995. The Asian Women's Human Rights Council and the Lila Pilipina, former comfort women, dress in black when they gather outside the Japanese embassy in Manila demanding compensation for the wartime crime of sexual slavery by the Japanese Army in World War II.

At the 1995 UN World Conference on Women in Beijing, over three thousand WIB held a vigil calling for "a world safer for women" and an end to wars and armed conflicts. Since 1996, Women in Black in Nepal have stood in silent vigils around the issues of trafficking and violence against women in public places in Katmandu. In 1998 and 1999, Women in Black groups demonstrated globally against US military maneuvers, which included continued sanctions and bombing raids against Iraq.

In 2000 the Coalition of Women for a Just Peace formed in Israel, where it joined Women in Black with nine other women's peace organizations. Thousands of women participate in mass Women in Black vigils twice a year in Israel. Over five thousand women in Cape Town, South Africa, demonstrated in 2001 on the eve of the World Court of Women Against War/For Peace. Women in Black in South Africa stood against war and for peace.

Since 2002, WIB groups everywhere have been actively opposing any extension of military action by the United States and allied governments, of attacks on particular states, notably Iraq. In 2003 at the Asia Social Forum in Hyderabad, over three thousand women dressed in black protested against Israel's Occupation of Palestine, the war on Iraq, and war crimes of the United States.

Nationally and internationally, Women in Black have received awards for their work for peace. The worldwide network was awarded the Millennium Women's Peace Prize sponsored by the NGO International Alert and the UN agency UNIFEM. And the following year, the network was a nominee for the Nobel Peace Prize. The network has also been honored by Church Women United, USA. Donne in Nero was awarded the Gold Dove of Peace, an Italian prize, in 2002. Israeli Women in

Black won the Aachen Peace Prize (1991), the peace award of the city of San Giovanni d'Asso in Italy (1994), and the Jewish Peace Fellowship's Peacemaker Award (2001).

It is estimated that more than 150 Women in Black groups exist in at least twenty-four countries. WIB is not an organization but a means of communicating with silent vigils against any evidence of violence, militarism, or war. Void of any constitution, Women in Black is a worldwide momentum without movement of women in black standing still for peace.

Sources:

http://www.womeninblack.org/old/en/history.
http://www.womeninblack.org/old/en/about.
http://www.carolforpeace.com/women_in_black.html.
December 2007

Sarah Frances Whiting, - Physics Professor/Meteorologist
Public Domain

Joanne Simpson - First PhD in Meteorology/Weather Satellite
NASA Public Domain

Dr. Mary Edwards Walker– Surgeon Only
Female Medal of Honor Recipient
Public Domain

Fanny Mendelssohn, Composer/Pianist
Courtesy Public Domain

Florence Beatrick Price – Symphonic Composer
Courtesy Special Collection, University of
Arkansas Libraries, Fayetteville

Attny. Lyda Conley – Native
American Indian Activist
Public Domain

Eva Perón – First Lady of Argentina
Archivo Grafico de la Nación
Public Domain

Tammy Baldwin
U.S. Representative & U.S. Senator
Courtesy GovTrack.us

Florence PragKahn, U.S. Representative
Courtesy Library of Congress

Nellie Tayloe Ross, First Elected Female U.S. Govenor
George Grantham Bain Collection
Courtesy Library of Congress
Public Domain

First-First Lady Martha Washington
Courtesy of National First Ladiess' Library
Public Domain

Michelle Obama
First-First Lady Descendent of U.S. Plantation Slavery
Courtesy Library of Congress

Edna White – Classical Trumpet Player, Bandleader, Composer
Courtesy ©Susan Fleet, trumpeter, author, music historian
: http://susanfleet.com/

Frida Kahlo – Painter
Photographer: Guillermo Kahlo
Public Domain

Yoshiko Uchida, Author
Courtesy of The Bancroft Library, University of California Berkeley

Rosa Parks – Civil Rights Icon
Corbis Image

Wilma ManKiller - First Female Cherokee Nation Chief
Courtesy: J Pat Carter – www.jpatcarter.me

Rosa González, RN c.1916
Public Domain

MariaTeresa Ríos Versace
Image in Pitt Summer 1948 XXIII, p15
Courtesy of University Library System, University of Pittsburgh

Maurine Watkins - 1920s Chicago Tribune Columnist
Photo by Vandamm Studio© Billy Rose Theatre Division,
The New York Public Library for the Performing Arts

Sr. M. Francis Borgia, O.S.F. (2nd row from top center)
Maria von Trapp (shown to the right of Sr.)
Courtesy of the Alvernia Alumnae Association-Sr.Kate Brenner

Chapter Thirty-Six
Phyllisharmonic
~

*F*anny Mendelssohn published six of her own songs under the name of Felix Mendelssohn, the brother she idolized, as he did her. As young children, the talents of both brother and sister were evident. When Fanny was eleven and Felix seven, they had four music teachers. At age thirteen, she could play *The Well-Tempered Clavier* in its entirety by memory, and that same year, Felix began to perform in public. He was nine. She was a girl. The year was 1818. Her public piano debut did not happen until twenty years hence.

Fanny had received disconcerting disapproval from her father against performing as a professional musician. And while Felix appreciated her profound composing talents, he was unable to support any publication of her compositions because she was a woman. Their beliefs were entrenched in the culture of their time.

Without support and encouragement, Fanny wanted to promote herself into a public arena that did not welcome her gender—though it appreciated her music, under her brother's name. In 1846, Felix had a private audience with Queen Victoria, who liked his songs, especially, *Italien* from his Op. 8 collection. Felix royally admitted it was not his but his sister's.

As was the queen's, the public's knowledge of Fanny Mendelssohn and her compositions is all but naught. Though she composed 466 pieces, most are unpublished, some in private family archives. Her songs, especially her "songs without words," piano pieces in the style of the Lied, a favorite genre for her brother, who is often credited with its invention, though the credit well might be his sister's.

Fanny Mendelssohn died suddenly at age forty-two. Deeply affected, Felix lost consciousness, never fully recovered, and died six months later.

Clara Wieck was twenty when she penned these thoughts: "I once thought that I possessed a creative talent, but I have given up that idea: a woman must not desire to be a composer, not one has done it, and why should I expect to?" The year was 1839.

Clara, a child protégé, was only nine when she performed her first public piano concert. When eighteen, among European pianists, she was second only to Franz Liszt. She had introduced Chopin's music to Germany and was the first to play Beethoven's *Appassionata Sonata* in Berlin.

She introduced many of Robert Schumann's works to the public and, at age twenty-seven, married him. She bore him seven children in sixteen years. Meanwhile, she continued to pursue a piano career. While she edited and promoted Schumann's compositions, she also introduced many works of Johannes Brahms to the public. Brahms, who never married, was said to have been in love with Clara. He respected her musical judgment and valued her criticism.

But Clara doubted her own creative ability and barely composed after her marriage. Her doubts, undoubtedly, were deeply rooted in the culture of her time. A leading critic wrote, "Reproductive genius can be admitted to the pretty sex, but productive genius unconditionally cannot ... there will never be a woman composer ... I do not believe in the feminine form of the word 'creator.'"

Had her culture valued feminist values, Clara might not have kept her creative talents composed. She might have composed creative and talented compositions, exponentially. Clara Wieck Schumann died in 1896.

At the age of four, Florence Beatrice Smith performed her first piano recital in Little Rock, Arkansas. At age eleven, her first musical composition was published. After high school, she entered the New England Conservatory, where she began to seriously consider music composition.

After receiving her degree in 1906, Professor Smith taught music in Arkansas at the Cotton Plant-Arkadelphia Academy, at Shorter College, and at Clark University in Atlanta. In 1912, she taught privately in Little Rock, became active in composition, and married attorney Thomas J.

Price. In the 1920s, the couple and their two daughters moved to Chicago. When her marriage dissolved, Price and her daughters endured difficult financial circumstances.

In 1929, Price composed her first ambitious work for piano, *Fantasie Nègre*. It combines Negro melodies and rhythms with classical European forms and techniques. Price performed competitively as a way to achieve recognition and pay bills. Her four winning categories included the top prize for a symphonic composition in the 1932 Wanamaker Competition.

Frederick Stock, then conductor of the Chicago Symphony Orchestra, presented Price's Symphony in E Minor for the Chicago World's Fair in 1933. It was the first time a symphony written by a black woman had been performed by a major symphony orchestra. Critics raved.

Price composed well into her fifties, completing over three hundred works. Her songs and arrangements were performed by famous artists, which included Marian Anderson. Her symphonies and chamber works were known for the melodies she adapted from Negro spirituals and are considered a vital component of the New Negro Arts Movement. Florence Beatrice Price died of a stroke in Chicago in 1953.

Sources:

Carol Plantamura, *Women Composers*.

Women Making Music, Ed. Jane Boers and Judith Tick.

http://www.wwnorton.com/college/music/enj9/shorter/composers/ hensel.htm.

http://chevalierdesaintgeorges.homestead.com/Price.html.

April 2008

Chapter Thirty-Seven
Rhythm and Gender

*I*n Spain, the twelfth day of Christmas is celebrated by drummers drumming in the feast of the Epiphany each January 6. This tradition, well documented in "The Twelve Days of Christmas" song that sings twelve drummers drumming, has its roots in Christian doctrine.

The song is an English Christmas carol with two levels of meaning for Roman Catholics who were banned from openly practicing their faith in England from 1558 until 1829. Each element in the carol has a code word for the religious reality unable to be spoken, or sung, openly. Similarly and spiritually women were banned from drumming.

As a young girl, Layne Redmond (1952–2013) wanted to be a drummer, but was told by her parents that drumming was for boys. In her book, *When the Drummers Were Women* (1997), Redmond writes that the earliest known religious rituals revolved around the beat of frame drums. Women, considered holy because of their seemingly magical ability to create new life, performed these sacred drumming rituals. Historian William H. McNeill suggested that the rhythmic rites associated with the ancient goddesses were critical prerequisites for the emergence of humanity. Goddess drumming was a powerful tool for communal bonding until the fall of the Roman Empire.

Evidence points to major incursions of warlike nomads, invaders referred to as Kurgans or Aryans or Indo-Europeans who rode horse-drawn chariots and brandished swords. The peaceful goddess-based cultures were no match for them. In *The Chalice and the Blade* (1987), Riane Eisler describes Kurgan culture as a dominator model of social organization in which "male dominance, male violence, and a generally hierarchic and authoritarian social structure was the norm."

The fall of the Roman Empire marks the powerful transition point in history from the worship of many gods and goddesses into the worship of one. And that one was a god. The goddess was demonized, imbued with evil connotations, and essentially, buried. The new power elite doomed the goddess to eventual oblivion—erased this culture. Rhythmic music, perhaps an echo of the human pulse, was central to these women's rites, and the drum was the core of the rhythm. But the warriors of this new deity banned the sacred frame drum.

The drum was silenced but not the drummer. She still drums in women who pulsate for women and women's causes.

And the beat goes on.

Sources:

http://www.timeanddate.com/holidays/common/epiphany.

http://www.catholicnewsagency.com/resources/advent/customs-and-traditions/the-history-of-the-twelve-days-of-christmas/.

http://wildhunt.org/2013/10/layne-redmond-1952-2013.html.

Layne Redmond, *When the Drummers Were Women*.

January 2005

Chapter Thirty-Eight
Lyda Oh Lyda
~

*L*yda Conley was a lawyer when women, especially Native American women, were not supposed to be lawyers. The year was 1909. And not only was Conley a lawyer, she was a lawyer who challenged the US government in court—and not just any court, the US Supreme Court. When the federal government sought to develop the Huron Place Cemetery land, she argued that, by law, Native American burial grounds were sacred and entitled to federal protection.

Conley was of the Wyandot Nation, a well-educated, prosperous people of prominent lawyers, businessmen, abolitionists, suffragettes, and women of strength and courage. They had long lived and prospered in Ohio on 110,000 acres of prime agricultural and forest acreage. Some of the land had been given to them in payment for the intelligence services they had provided to colonial forces during the Revolutionary War. But it was now 1830, the era of the 1830 US Indian Removal Act, which led to the infamous Trail of Tears, and the white settlers coveted this land. For thirteen years, the Wyandots had strongly resisted removal. But, they were removed.

Approximately seven hundred Wyandots were forced to the Kansas wilderness territories of the Great Plains west of the Missouri River. While they were encamped on the east banks of the Missouri, where they were held during a summer of flooding and disease, as well as through the winter and spring of 1844, many died. Their bodies were carried across the river into Kansas Territory to be buried in Huron Park, a 1.9-acre plot granted the Wyandot by the US government. Most were buried according to tribal custom, wrapped in their blankets in unmarked graves. Thus, the Huron Place Cemetery was established.

The Wyandots accepted their fate and began to establish a new life centered around the small cemetery. Streets were built and a town developed as a center of business and commerce. In 1855 the government offered citizenship to those Wyandots whom they deemed ready to join the white society. At least sixty-nine of those so deemed did not take the United States' offer to relinquish their tribal status and identity in exchange for citizenship. Among them was Hannah Zane, grandmother of Lyda, and Lyda's mother, then a minor.

Those who accepted were migrated from Kansas to Oklahoma. This divided the Wyandot Nation into the Wyandot of Kansas and the Wyandotte of Oklahoma and divided their land in Kansas. But the sacred burying ground remained intact.

Eventually, Kansas City's growth surrounded the cemetery, and by 1906, developers wanted to expand on this prime property. The US citizen Wyandottes in Oklahoma approved sale of the cemetery for development. Congress then authorized the sale with proceeds to go to the U.S. citizen Wyandottes in Oklahoma.

Conley and her two sisters, Ida and Lena, strongly disagreed with the proposed sale and announced they would protect the graves of their ancestors, with shotguns if necessary. Their mother was buried there, as were their sister, Sarah, many cousins, aunts, uncles, their grandmother Hannah Zane, and countless others. The three sisters marched to the cemetery, built a six-by-eight-foot frame shack, moved in, and defended the cemetery for more than three years.

Throughout this period, Lyda, who had graduated from Kansas City School of Law in 1902 (one of four women of the of sixty-seven to graduate) and who was the first woman admitted to the Kansas Bar, prepared herself for legal action by an assiduous study of law books to better contest the government order. It was a unique legal situation. The rightful ownership of the cemetery between the two Wyandot Nations was in doubt. But only one group had federal recognition for the legality that was to be solved by the Department of Justice.

The Wyandot were a matriarchal and matrilineal society, with women influential in all matters of business and politics. Remember that Conley's grandmother had refused to choose between becoming a citizen or being deemed "incompetent," and Conley's mother had denied the government's wish that she become a citizen, albeit the government's wish did prevail.

As a young woman, Lyda rowed a boat across the Missouri River every day to attend Park College in Missouri. Lyda was widely read and traveled, and she corresponded with many beyond Kansas City. At a time when no women (and really no one period) were supposed to challenge the powerful or articulate legal theories (theories minority people were not allowed to assert) Lyda did both.

In 1907, Conley filed a petition in the US Circuit Court for the District of Kansas for injunction against the government's authorization of sale. The court ruled against Conley, so she appealed. The case went to the Supreme Court of the United States, where Conley was allowed to argue the case. US Supreme Court Justice Oliver Wendell Holmes ruled in favor of the lower courts that the government's proposed action was legal. Conley petitioned for a rehearing. Her petition was denied in 1910. After nearly three years of litigation, Conley had lost. The path again was cleared, at least legally, for the sale of the Huron Place Cemetery.

But Conley's passionate fight to save the cemetery was far from over. Lyda Conley would not admit defeat. She and her sister Lena continued their guard together after the death of their sister Ida. Though their fence was torn down repeatedly, the sisters rebuilt it, repeatedly. (It was rumored that, in the middle of many nights, townspeople would come to help rebuild the fence.)

Then, on July 29, 1910, federal marshals acting under a court order entered the Huron Place Cemetery and destroyed their shack. Undaunted, the two women rebuilt it. It would be destroyed and rebuilt at least twice more before federal officials would give up. The physical presence of the sisters and the notoriety of the lawsuit had dissuaded potential buyers, and the commission established to find a buyer eventually gave up.

Conley's activities attracted nationwide attention, including that of Kansas Senator Charles Curtis (to be Herbert Hoover's vice president). A

Topekan of Kaw descent, Curtis visited the Huron Place Cemetery in 1912 and, soon after, introduced a bill in Congress to preclude the sale of the cemetery. In 1913, Congress approved his legislation, recommended the cemetery become a national monument, and appropriated $10,000 for its renovation and preservation.

In 1918, Conley sought an injunction to restrain city officials from completing renovations and improvements she believed were being done carelessly, without regard for the presence of unmarked graves. In June 1937, Conley chased some people from the cemetery and was charged with disturbance. A young judge gave her choice of a ten-dollar fine for disturbing the peace or a ten-day jail sentence. Conley served the sentence with pride.

For the rest of their lives, Lyda and Lena watched over and protected the Wyandot graves at the Huron Place Cemetery. They were arrested on several occasions on various charges relating to their attempts to interfere with city officials whose actions, the Conleys believed, were desecrating Wyandot graves. Those who knew the Conley sisters in their later years have attested that they spent much of their time in the cemetery, close to the graves of their ancestors, watching over them and honoring their spirits.

Lyda Conley died at age seventy-two on May 28, 1946. Within months of her death, the federal government and the Wyandotte Tribe of Oklahoma again initiated efforts to move the Wyandot graves and sell the cemetery land. In 1947, separate bills were introduced in the House and Senate, but neither was enacted. Nine years later, Congress enacted legislation to terminate federal supervision over the Wyandot Tribe and explicitly authorized the sale of the cemetery as part of the termination process.

By 1957, the Oklahoma Wyandottes threatened to move the bodies from Huron Place to a site in Oklahoma. Local businesses were eager to play a part in the destruction of Huron Place Cemetery. But no federal money had been appropriated to pay for the disinterments, and the plans for Huron Place languished.

On September 15, 1958, Lena, the last of the four daughters of Eliza Burton Zane Conley and Andrew Syrenus Conley, died in her home in

Kansas City, Kansas. Three days later, she was laid to rest near the graves of her mother, father, and three sisters. The tombstone that she herself designed to mark her grave bears her birth name; her Indian name Floating Voice; and the warning, "Cursed be the villain that molest their graves." Even in death, it seemed, the Conley sisters were unwilling to give up their fight to protect the cemetery and what it represented.

In 1959, the city of Kansas City, Kansas, and descendants of the US citizen Wyandots initiated separate lawsuits against the United States and the Wyandottes of Oklahoma, seeking to invalidate the termination legislation authorizing the sale of the Huron Place Cemetery. A three-judge panel of the district court found unanimously that the descendants lacked standing to bring an action concerning the Treaty of 1855. The Supreme Court summarily affirmed this decision in 1961. However, despite failure in federal court, the cemetery was not sold—for it had come to be regarded as a local historic landmark, and as in 1910, no buyers were forthcoming.

In 1971, after a sixty-five-year legal battle to protect this sacred burial ground, preservation groups succeeded in having the Huron Place Cemetery listed on the National Register of Historic Places, acknowledged by a small wooden sign and a series of bronze plaques. Although this status does not render the cemetery absolutely protected against encroachment or desecration, it is extremely unlikely that the cemetery will ever again face a realistic threat of destruction.

In 2008, actor Ben Kingsley announced plans to produce *Whispers Like Thunder*, an SBK Pictures film about the epic story of the Huron Place Cemetery and the Native American women who struggled to preserve it.

The mission of Lyda Conley to preserve Huron Place Cemetery appears, at last, to be complete. It is where Lyda Burton Conley, Kansas attorney and direct descendant of the great Wyandot Chief Tarhe, is buried near her family at the Wyandot Burying Ground, the Huron Place Cemetery.

Sources:

> *"Trespassers, Beware!: Lyda Burton Conley and the Battle for Huron Place Cemetery,"* Kim Dayton, Yale Journal of Law and Feminism,

1996, at Women's Legal History, Stanford University, accessed 25 Feb 2009.

Ben Kingsley's SBK announces, Variety 17. November 2008.

http://www.variety.com/article/VR1117996028.html?categoryid =13&cs=1.

http://www.morofilms.com/index_sub_whispers.html.

http://en.wikipedia.org/wiki/Lyda_Conley.

October/November 2010

Chapter Thirty-Nine
Of Married Men and Mistresses
~

*D*ocumentation exists that Thomas Jefferson, framer of the US Constitution, forefather, lawyer, third president of the United States, and slave owner, fathered at least one illegitimate child with his house slave, Sally Hemings, if not all six of her children. These allegations have long been regarded as fact by the Hemings family line. The November 1998 scientific journal *Nature* reported that DNA results established "'beyond a reasonable doubt' that Jefferson fathered Eston Hemings," resolving a controversy two centuries old.

Early nineteenth-century rumors of the alleged affair noted that Jefferson and Hemings were living in the same household when her children were conceived, and there was a strong resemblance between Hemings's children and the children of Jefferson's wife Martha. Rumors were further substantiated citing that Hemings's slave children were given special privileges in the house at Monticello and that Jefferson had established that their freedom be granted upon his death.

New York Law School professor Annette Gordon-Reed, author of *Thomas Jefferson and Sally Hemings: An American Controversy*, quotes a letter by Jefferson in which he wrote; "that he considered female slaves to be far more valuable than male slaves. Why? Because female slaves had children and, thus, added to capital." Gordon-Reed also argued that "establishment historians had deliberately avoided examining evidence about the relationship."

Maria Eva Duarte Perón's father, Juan Duarte, had two families—one with his legal wife, Adela D'Huart, with whom he had several children, and another with his mistress, Juana Ibarguren. Evita was the fifth child born to his mistress. Duarte belonged to an influential family in Chivilcoy, Argentina. He was a prosperous and prestigious leader in politics and was named Deputy Justice of the Peace in 1908. Duarte did not hide the fact that he had two families and divided his time between them. But eventually, he abandoned his mistress and their children, leaving them with nothing more than a paper formally recognizing the children as his. When he died in a 1925 car accident, he left his mistress and his illegitimate children financially pauperized. They were denied any inheritance. Evita was six years old at the time. In 1934, at the age of fifteen, she went to Buenos Aires to find work and begin her career.

After his New York to Paris, solo flight in May 1927, Charles Lindbergh was ready to move on from stunt flying, barnstorming, and competitive racing to serious flight explorations. He wanted to marry, and he wanted to marry a healthy woman who liked flying, because he wanted his wife to be his flying companion on future expeditions he had planned. He set his sights on Anne Morrow, daughter of the US ambassador to Mexico, and invited her to go flying when they first met. He let her experience the controls (her first flight training?). When she told him she wanted to learn to fly - he smiled. They married in May 1929. Anne was critical to the success of Charles's flights. She was his copilot, radio operator, and navigator.

Together, they had four children. Together, they purchased a home in Connecticut. Together, they authored many books. Their youngest daughter, Reeve said, they wrote not in collaboration but in mutual awareness and with mutual support. Of Anne's fourteen books, *A Gift from the Sea*, printed in forty-five languages, sold over three million copies. Charles's *Spirit of St. Louis* earned him a Pulitzer Prize.

Charles continued his aeronautic work and was away from Anne and the children most of the last two decades of his life. During this period, he was silent about his whereabouts; she remained a subservient and devoted wife. But she also discovered her independence, grew her confidence, and became head of her household. In the late 1960s, Charles became a more integral part of their marriage and he and Anne again began to travel together.

In 1974, with Anne by his side, Charles died of cancer. In 2001, Anne, age ninety-four and frail, surrounded by family and friends, died peacefully. In 2003, it became public that Charles had seven grown children in Europe, conceived and birthed by three women, each to whom he had written a letter from his deathbed requesting "utmost secrecy."

Former president of France, Francois Mitterrand's "second family" was revealed to the public in 1994, a year before he left office. He had a state apartment where he had installed his mistress, an art curator, under heavy police guard. At the time, most of France believed the secretive Socialist leader (1981–95), was living with Danielle, his wife, at their Left Bank home.

Mitterrand was well known in Paris as a profound womanizer. At what stage Danielle became aware of this twenty-year liaison is not known. But a daughter, Mazarine, was born in 1974 to Annie Pingeot, a campaign volunteer twenty years younger than Mitterrand, who was then sixty-two. At a breakfast with senior French journalists in 1984, Mitterrand admitted that he had an illegitimate daughter. "So what?" he challenged the journalists. None printed this story.

When Mitterrand underwent cancer surgery in 1994, Pingeot secretly occupied the hospital room next to his. Mazarine, his illegitimate child, kept in the shadows for almost two decades, was ousted in 1996 as her father lay dying, and she faced an abstruse future after an abstruse past. According to author Phillippe Alexandre, Mitterrand's legitimate son, Jean-Christophe, and Mazarine met in a hospital corridor when both were visiting their father after his cancer surgery. Jean-Christophe snubbed her and is said to have told friends, "As long as my father doesn't speak of this young woman, for me she doesn't exist."

In 2005, Mazarine Marie Pingeot-Mitterrand, thirty-four, told *The Sunday Times*, "For 19 years I was nobody's daughter, but I've finally decided to add my father's name to my identity papers."

Sources:

Annette Gordon-Reed, *Thomas Jefferson and Sally Hemings: An American Controversy.*

Kathleen C. Winters, *Anne Morrow Lindbergh: First Lady of the Air.*

Reeve Lindbergh, "Secrets and Lives," *MORE*, March 2008.

http://latinamericanhistory.about.com/od/historyofsouthamerica/a/evita.htm.

http://www.evitaperon.org/part1.htm.

https://en.wikipedia.org/wiki/François_Mitterrand.

June 2011

Chapter Forty
Fab Forty-Four SenateHers
~

*F*orty-four, 44, XLIV—regardless of how it is stated, written, spoken, and/or numerically noted, as few as 44 female senators have legislatively served in the 224-year history of the United States of America. During that same 224-year history, in that same country, one thousand nine hundred and two, 1,902, MCMII, regardless of how it is stated, written, spoken and/or numerically noted, as many as 1,902 male senators have legislatively served.

In a country whose people's gender percentage is fifty, 50, L men and, fifty, 50, L women, no matter how it is stated, written, spoken, and/or numerically noted - in a country of the people, by the people and for the people - in a country which purports to be a nation of laws, including voting laws, the people have elected forty-four female senate legislators from twenty-six states, and one thousand nine hundred and two male senate legislators from fifty states* As to a 50 percent gender-equitable US Senate of Women and Men representation one day? You can vote on it.

Twenty-four states have yet to send women to the United States Senate. They are Arizona, Colorado, Connecticut, Delaware, Idaho, Indiana, Iowa, Kentucky, Mississippi, Montana, Nevada, New Jersey, New Mexico, Ohio, Oklahoma, Pennsylvania, Rhode Island, South Carolina, Tennessee, Utah, Vermont, Virginia, West Virginia, and Wyoming.

Celebrate the "Fab Forty-Four" and their twenty-six states in this time line, from 1922-2013:

1. Rebecca Latimer Felton – Georgia
2. Hattie Wyatt Caraway – Arkansas

3. Rose McConnell Long – Louisiana
4. Dixie Bibb Graves – Alabama
5. Gladys Pyle – South Dakota
6. Vera Cahalan Bushfield – South Dakota
7. Margaret Chase Smith – Maine
8. Eva Kelley Bowring – Nebraska
9. Hazel Hempel Abel – Nebraska
10. Maurine Brown Neuberger – Oregon
11. Elaine Schwartzenburg Edwards – Louisiana
12. Muriel Humphrey – Minnesota
13. Maryon Allen – Alabama
14. Nancy Landen Kassebaum – Kansas
15. Paula Hawkins – Florida
16. Barbara Mikulski – Maryland
17. Jocelyn Burdick – North Dakota
18. Dianne Feinstein – California
19. Barbara Boxer – California
20. Carol Mosley Braun – Illinois
21. Patty Murray – Washington
22. Kay Bailey Hutchinson – Texas
23. Olympia Jean Snowe – Maine
24. Sheila Frahm – Kansas
25. Mary Landrieu – Louisiana
26. Susan Collins – Maine
27. Blanche Lincoln – Arkansas
28. Debbie Stabenow – Michigan
29. Jean Carnahan – Missouri
30. Hillary Rodham Clinton – New York
31. Maria Cantwell – Washington
32. Lisa Murkowski – Alaska
33. Elizabeth Dole – North Carolina
34. Amy Klobuchar – Minnesota
35. Claire McCaskill – Missouri
36. Kay Hagan – North Carolina

37. Jeanne Shaheen – New Hampshire
38. Kristen Gillibrand – New York
39. Kelly Ayotte – New Hampshire
40. Tammy Baldwin – Wisconsin
41. Deb Fisher – Nebraska
42. Heidi Heitkamp – North Dakota
43. Maize Hirono – Hawaii
44. Elizabeth Warren – Massachusetts

TOTAL NUMBER OF US SENATORS   1789 TO PRESENT - 1,946
TOTAL NUMBER OF US MALE SENATORS   1789 TO PRESENT - 1,902
TOTAL NUMBER OF US FEMALE SEATORS 1789 TO PRESENT -   44

Further "fab" information on each of the Fab Forty-Four female senators is just a click away. Visit this link to learn more about these women who have served and legislated for the men and women of the United States of America: http://www.senate.gov/artandhistory/history/common/briefing/women_senators.htm

Note: In 2013, President Barack Obama initiated dinner meetings with lawmakers seeking bipartisan compromise on key issues. One dinner took place with a dozen senate Democrats, and two similar dinners with senate Republicans. Subsequently, New York Senator Kirsten Gillibrand initiated and suggested to Mr. Obama a dinner meeting with the twenty (20, XX) women senators representing both parties who currently served in the Senate. She invited Mr. Obama to one of the women senators' regularly scheduled monthly dinners held at one of their homes. Mr. Obama welcomed the idea but not the invitation and, instead, invited the women senators to the White House for a dinner he hosted on Tuesday, April 23, 2013.

Source:
    http://www.senate.gov/artandhistory/history/resources/pdf/chronlist.pdf.
May 2013

Chapter Forty-One
House Women

~

*F*orty-four, 44, XLIV, of the fifty, 50, L, United States have sent women to serve in the US House of Representatives since the US Congress first convened on March 4, 1789. It would be another 128 years after congress first convened for women's place in the House to begin when the first woman was elected to this chamber. The six, 6, VI, states of the fifty United States still to elect a woman representative to serve in the House are Alaska, Delaware, Iowa, Mississippi, North Dakota, and Vermont.

In the 224-year history of the United States of America, in a country whose people are gender equitably split equitably, fifty, 50, L, men, and, fifty, 50, L, women; in a country of the people, by the people, and for the people; in a country which purports to be a nation of laws, including voting laws; the people have elected a total of 10,814 representatives to serve in the House. Of that total, 10,614 representatives have been men, and 200 have been women.

The first of these two hundred House women, Jeannette Rankin elected by the men and women of Montana in 1917, said, "I may be the first woman member of Congress but I won't be the last." Rankin was elected again in 1940 and is the only member of Congress to have voted against the United States' entry into World War I and World War II. The percentage of women during Rankin's first term as the only woman in the Sixty-Fifth Congress was 0.2 percent. During her second term in the Seventy-Sixth Congress, seven more women were elected and the percentage of House women was 1.8 percent. A few more "firsts" of the first two hundred women follow.

Florence Prag Kahn of California in 1925, the first Jewish woman to serve, did so with one other woman in the Sixty-Ninth Congress establishing a women's percentage 0.7 percent.

Katharine St. George of New York state elected in 1946, served in the Seventy-Ninth Congress with ten other women creating a 2.5 percentage of House women. In 1962, St. George was the first (female or male) lawmaker to propose legislation ensuring gender equal pay for equal work. Staunchly opposed, despite ardent support, from groups such as the American Association of University Women (AAUW), it failed. The bill was reintroduced by fellow House woman Edith Green and passed as the 1963 Equal Pay Act.

Ruth Thompson was elected from Michigan to the Eighty-Second Congress, bringing the total of female representation to 2.3 percent. Thompson was subsequently reelected to the two succeeding Congresses and served from 1951 to 1957. She was the first woman to serve on the House Judiciary Committee, the preeminent committee charged with overseeing the administration of justice at the federal level and responsible for impeachments of federal officials.

Patsy Mink of Hawaii, third generation Japanese (Sansei) and first House woman minority member, was elected in 1965 to the Eighty-Ninth Congress, and female House representation was 2.5 percent. Mink authored the Title IX legislation and the Women's Educational Equity Act and introduced the first comprehensive Early Childhood Education Act. These laws were declared landmark laws by Congress as they advanced gender equality rights in America beyond what was imagined at the time. Title IX was renamed in her honor.

Shirley Chisholm of New York state, the first African American House woman, was elected in 1968 to the Ninetieth Congress. But the House remained 2.5 percent female. Chisholm served continuously to the Ninety-Seventh Congress where female representation temporarily reached a paltry 4.8 percent.

Geraldine Ferraro was elected to the Ninety-Fifth Congress (4.1 percent female) in 1978 by the state of New York. She became the first woman vice presidential candidate for a major American political party as the 1984 running mate to presidential candidate Walter Mondale.

Louise Slaughter, also of New York state, was elected in 1987 and joined the Hundredth Congress (5.3 percent female). She was the first woman chair of the powerful House Rules Committee. Slaughter coauthored the Violence Against Women Act in 1994 and wrote legislation to make permanent the United States Department of Justice's Violence Against Women Office.

Nancy Pelosi of California, also elected in 1987, became the first woman House minority whip, the first female House minority leader, and the first woman to serve as Speaker of the House—in the 110th and 111th Congresses. At the time, Pelosi noted that her election to her role as "Speaker" broke the marble ceiling for all women. To date, she is the highest-ranking female politician in America's history.

Lleana Ros-Lehtinen of Florida was the first Hispanic woman (and the first Cuban American woman) to serve in the House. She was elected in 1989 to the 101st Congress, which was 6.7 percent female. In 2012, she was the first of her party in the House to fully support same-sex marriage.

Tammy Baldwin, Wisconsin's first openly gay/lesbian politician, was elected to the House in 1999 and joined the 106th Congress (13.3 percent female). As a member of the Wisconsin state legislature in 1994, Baldwin had pioneered a proposal legalizing same-sex marriage and proposed domestic partnerships in Wisconsin. In 2012, Baldwin became the first openly gay US Senator in history.

Mazie Hirono, elected from Hawaii in 2007 to the 110th Congress (17.2 percent female), is the first Buddhist House woman.

Judy May Chu of California was elected in 2009 to the current (as of this writing) 113th Congress (17.9 percent female) of 78 women serving with 357 men. Chu, the first Chinese House woman, introduced a resolution that formally expresses the regret of the House for the Chinese Exclusion Act of 1923, which imposed virtually total restrictions on Chinese immigration and naturalization and denied Chinese Americans basic freedoms because of their ethnicity. In 2012, it was only the fourth time the US Congress issued an apology to a group of people.

The votes of two hundred House women notably did matter legislatively, as did the votes that elected two hundred women into the House—emboldening its female membership from 0.2 percent to 17.9 percent. As to a 50 percent/50 states gender-equitable House men/House women representation one day? You can vote on it!

TOTAL NUMBER OF US REPRESENTATIVES	10,814
TOTAL NUMBER OF MALE US REPRESENTATIVES	10,614
TOTAL NUMBER OF FEMALE US REPRESENTATIVES	200

Sources and further fabulous facts on these two hundred House women can be found at these government links:

http://history.house.gov/Institution/Total-Members/Total-Members/ and

http://en.wikipedia.org/wiki/Women_in_the_United_States_House_of_Representatives.

June 2013

Chapter Forty-Two
GovernHers

*T*wenty-five states and the Commonwealth of Puerto Rico have elected thirty-six women as governors of their states. The six of those states that have elected more than one woman governor, their cumulative fifteen women governors profiled below, are Arizona (four), Texas (three), New Hampshire (two), Connecticut (two), Washington (two), and Kansas (2). Wyoming has elected one female governor and she was the first.

Wyoming

Nellie Tayloe Ross of Wyoming was the first woman elected governor of any US state. She was sworn into the office in 1925 after winning a special election to complete the term of her husband, who died during his term as governor.

Arizona – elected four women governors

Rose Mofford, as Arizona's first woman governor, returned stability to state politics after she was sworn into office in 1988 following the tumultuous impeachment of her predecessor, Evan Mecham. She did not run for reelection.

Jane Dee Hull, Arizona's second woman governor, completed the term of another male governor dishonorably removed from office when Governor Fife Symington was convicted of a felony and had to resign. Hull was sworn into office in 1997 by the first woman US Supreme Court Justice Sandra Day O'Connor, herself an Arizonian. Hull's successful reelection in 1998 was historic because for the first (and last) time in the 224-year history of the United States, all five of the top elected executive offices in one state were held by women—along with Governor Hull were Secretary of State Betsey Bayles, Attorney General Janet Napolitano, Treasurer Carol Springer, and Superintendent of Public Instruction Lisa Graham Keegan. Limited to eight consecutive years in office, Hull was constitutionally barred from running for a second full term in 2002 and was succeeded by Janet Napolitano.

Janet Napolitano was Arizona's third woman governor, and she served from 2003 to 2009. She was the first woman to succeed a woman governor and the first woman governor to win reelection. Earlier, in 1991, Napolitano had been an attorney for Anita Hill's sexual harassment testimony against Clarence Thomas in his US Supreme Court appointment proceedings. In 2009, after Napolitano was confirmed as the first woman secretary of Homeland Security, her term as governor was completed by Arizona Secretary of State Jan Brewer.

Jan Brewer, Arizona's fourth and third consecutive woman governor, went on to win the 2010 gubernatorial election with 55 percent of the vote and currently serves as Arizona's governor.

Texas – elected three women governors

Miriam "Ma" Ferguson was the twenty-ninth and thirty-second governor of Texas. Her colorful bio can be readily researched. First elected in 1925 and then again in 1932, she "almost" was the first female governor in the United States. But Nellie Tayloe Ross of Wyoming had been sworn into office two weeks prior.

Ann Richards was elected by the women and men of Texas as their second woman governor in 1991, sixty-six years after the governorship of "Ma" Ferguson. Richards came to national prominence with a keynote speech at the 1988 Democratic National Convention, in which she mentioned both George Bushes, H.W. and W. Her colorful quotes can be readily researched.

New Hampshire – elected two (but had three) women governors

Vesta Roy, as president of the state senate, assumed the governorship when Governor Hugh Gallen died in office. She served as acting governor for basically one month until Governor-elect John H. Sununu's inauguration in January 1983.

Jeanne Shaheen served as the first "elected" woman governor of New Hampshire from 1997–2003. She was the first woman in US history to be elected both as a governor and US senator. Shaheen was narrowly defeated by John Sununu in her first US Senate campaign in 2002. Criminal allegations of phone jamming Shaheen's campaign party lines that led to convictions and jail time for several men in Sununu's party may have contributed to her narrow loss. In her 2008 campaign, Shaheen defeated Sununu in a rematch and, as of this writing, is New Hampshire's senior US senator.

Maggie Hassen began her career in public service in 1999 when Governor Shaheen appointed her as a citizen adviser to the Advisory Committee to the Adequacy in Education and Finance Commission. Hassen, sworn into the New Hampshire governor's office for a two-year term in January 2013, was the last of the thirty-six women elected as governors in America to date.

Connecticut – elected two women governors

Ella Grasso, the first Connecticut woman governor, began her first term in 1975 and was then reelected to a second term in 1978. However, on December 31, 1980, she resigned due to ovarian cancer and died several weeks later at age sixty-one.

M. Jodi Rell became Connecticut's second female governor when Connecticut's Governor John G. Rowland resigned during another governor corruption investigation in 2004. In 2005, Rell signed into law a bill that made Connecticut the first state to adopt civil unions for same-sex couples without being directed to do so by a court. Rell was reelected in 2006. In 2009, she signed into law a gender-neutral marriage statute that also provided for civil unions to be automatically transformed into marriages on October 1, 2010.

Washington – elected two women governors

Dixy Lee Ray, elected in 1976, served one term as Washington's governor. Ray, a marine biologist, was appointed by Richard Nixon in 1973 as the first and only woman to chair the US Atomic Energy Commission. When Mount St. Helens' volcanic activity began after 123 years of dormancy, Governor Ray issued an executive order on April 3, 1980, that restricted area access. Her order, later credited by Forest Service responders of a post-eruption Warning and Response Survey, was noted as an order that kept between five and thirty thousand potential fatal victims out of the blast area when the volcanic eruptions began in May of 1980 and ended six years later.

Christine Gregoire was elected as Washington's second woman governor and served from 2004 to 2013. Governor Gregoire supported a number of important measures on car emission standards and unemployment benefits. She brokered new bipartisan transportation legislation, gave cost of living increases to state employees who hadn't received raises in "many years," and funded voter-approved initiatives to raise the pay of schoolteachers. It was suggested in the press that these groups gave money to fund her 2004 campaign. She signed a law granting same-sex couples domestic partnership rights on April 21, 2007, during her second term as Washington's governor.

Kansas – elected two women governors

Joan Finney, in 1991, was the first woman in the United States to defeat an incumbent governor in a general election. Kansas's oldest governor, at age sixty-five, Finney was one of the few pro-life governors of the time and did not seek reelection.

Kathleen Sebelius was the second woman governor of Kansas, and with her former governor of Ohio father, became the first father/daughter governor pair in the United States. Sebelius left her Kansas state senate seat when elected as the state insurance commissioner. For that campaign, she refused contributions from the insurance industry. She blocked the proposed merger of Blue Cross Blue Shield, Kansas's largest health insurer, with an Indiana-based company. It was the first time BCBS had been rebuffed in its acquisition attempts. Governor Sebelius served from 2003 to 2009, when she became the US secretary of Health and Human Services.

States where one woman has served as governor

Alabama, Kentucky, Vermont, Nebraska, Oregon, New Jersey, Ohio, Massachusetts, Montana, Puerto Rico, Delaware, Hawaii, Michigan, Utah, Louisiana, Alaska, North Carolina, New Mexico, South Carolina, Oklahoma, and Wyoming, previously as the first state to have a woman governor.

States where no women have served as governor

Arkansas, California, Colorado, Florida, Georgia, Idaho, Illinois, Indiana, Iowa, Main, Maryland, Minnesota, Mississippi, Missouri, Nevada, New York, North Dakota, Pennsylvania, Rhode Island, South Dakota, Tennessee, Virginia, West Virginia, and Wisconsin.

Will one day realize a more gender-equitable representation in terms of governorship in the United States? You can vote on it!

TOTAL NUMBER OF US GOVERNORS	1776 to present – 2,734
TOTAL NUMBER OF MALE US GOVERNORS	1776 to present – 2,698
TOTAL NUMBER OF FEMALE US GOVERNORS	1776 to present – 36

Sources:

https://en.wikipedia.org/wiki/List_of_female_governors
    _in_the_United_States

July 2013

Chapter Forty-Three
First First Ladies

~

Martha Washington was born Martha Dandridge on June 2, 1731, on her father's Virginia plantation near Williamsburg. At eighteen, she married the wealthy Daniel Parke Custis, two decades her senior. Eight years later, she was a young, wealthy widow with two children and independent control over her and her children's inheritances. Two years later, at her estate on the Pamunkey River northwest of Williamsburg known as the White House, George Washington (one year her junior) married Martha, the richest widow in Virginia. George won the presidency of the United States of America on April 14, 1789. Martha was to become the first First Lady of the United States of America.

Raised in an era when chattel slavery was legal in the American colonies (this was written in the US Constitution, Article I, Sections 2 and 9, and Article IV, Section 2), there is no record of Martha's questioning the inhumane institution of slavery. As part of her widow's "dower," Martha received at least eighty-five slaves. The full Custis Estate totaled about twenty-seven square miles of farm plantations, with 285 enslaved men, women, and children attached to those lands. Upon their marriage, George became the legal manager of the Custis Estate, but Martha continued to make many estate decisions. Using Martha's great wealth, George tripled the size of Mount Vernon.

George could not sell or own Martha's "dower" slaves, or the land they'd farmed for more than forty years, because they and the land were held in trust for Martha's son. Of the nine slaves George transported from his home in Virginia to work on the executive mansion in the Philadelphia capital, seven were Martha's "dower" slaves.

Abolition had begun in Pennsylvania, but nonresidents legally were allowed to hold slaves for up to six months. To prevent establishing residency for their enslaved workers, George and Martha rotated their house slaves in and out of Pennsylvania within the six-month legal guidelines. George reasoned that residency would have qualified them for manumission that could have left him liable to the Custis Estate for the monetary value of any enslaved people gone free.

First Lady Martha had promised a young female slave of hers, Ona Judge, as a gift to her granddaughter Eliza Custis. It is written that Martha was personally distraught upon learning Ona had escaped, hid with free black friends, and successfully traveled north. According to biographer Patricia Brady, Ona Judge professed a great regard for Martha and the way she had been treated, but she couldn't face a future as a slave for herself and her children. Another house slave, their chief cook, Hercules, also escaped. By 1797, the number of Martha's "dower" slaves had grown to 153, and Washington's slaves numbered 124.

George willed that his slaves be freed upon his death. However, because he was unable to own Martha's "dowers," he was not able to will them to be freed or rented to others, where they might have worked themselves free. Thus, to spare Martha from seeing their slave families torn apart, were any of her "dowers" to be sold individually by the estate, Washington's will also stated that his slaves not be sold until after Martha's death. George died suddenly in 1797. Four years later, alive and well, Martha freed his slaves.

Abigail Adams had visited Martha and noted a sinister motive for Martha having freed George's slaves while she was still alive. In a letter, Adams wrote, "With their freedom suspended until her death, she [Martha] did not feel as though her life was safe in their hands ... [for] it was in their interest to get rid of her." Martha died in 1801, willed her "dower" slaves to her four grandchildren, with Elisha, the one slave Martha owned outright, specifically bequeathed to her grandson.

Michelle Obama was born Michelle LaVaughn Robinson, on January 17, 1964, on the south side of Chicago, where her father was an employee of the city's water plant. In 1992, Barack Obama (three years her senior) married Michelle at a church on Chicago's south side when both were young lawyers with student loans from Harvard. Barack won the presidency of the United States of America on November 4, 2008. Michelle became the first First Lady of the United States of America, a First Lady who is a descendent of American plantation slavery.

Sources:

Henry Wiencek, *U.S. Constitution*; *An Imperfect God: George Washington, His Slaves, and the Creation of America.*
http://en.wikipedia.org/wiki/Martha_Washington.
http://www.biography.com/people/michelle-obama-307592.
November 2008

Chapter Forty-Four
Trumpeting Women

~

Wat happened to women trumpeters during the 318 years between 1655 and 1973 is worthy of note. Also worthy of note is that no anatomical gender difference exists to allow male and prevent female trumpeting. Still, trumpet opportunities historically excluded females as they promoted males. Not until 1973 did a major orchestra hire its first female principle trumpeter.

It is chronicled that Johanna Von Hoff was a Viennese trumpeter in the 1655 court of Emperor Leopold I and that J. Heneage Carter had an all-girl brass band in the 1860s in New England. Child prodigy Edna White had her first trumpet solo performance at Carnegie Hall in 1902. She was nine and promptly recruited to study at the newly founded Institute of Musical Art (now Julliard). At her commencement in 1907, she was the only graduate to perform a solo and the only graduate not to receive a degree, for which she was deemed too young.

Due to the rarity of wage-earning trumpeting engagements available to women, many women of the time created their own groups and employed other women. Edna formed her first all-woman trumpet quartet in 1910. But despite her talent, Julliard training, and rave reviews, few would hire all-women groups. After two years, Edna returned to Indianapolis and married.

Her husband disapproved of her trumpet playing, and Edna disapproved of his disapproval. However, when his foreign bank accounts were frozen because of World War I, he did not object when she formed her second all-woman trumpet quartet and became the family's source of income. After a pregnant pause in her career, Edna left her husband one year after the birth of their son. To support herself and Douglas, she formed the Edna White Brass Quartet and toured the vaudeville circuit throughout the 1920s.

Olivia Manetta Douroux and her husband Louis were trumpeters in Louisiana in the early 1900s. Louis played in a brass band but codes of feminine respectability restricted Olivia from playing in public. She could perform only at private parties, where it is written she played stunningly difficult trumpet duets with Louis.

Their thirteen-year-old daughter Dolly professionally played piano at Lulu White's Mahogany Hall. Although Dolly could play the trumpet, bass, drums, and guitar, it was as a pianist that she could perform publicly in 1917 to earn wages, but only for a while. In 1922, Dolly married Placide Adams who preferred his wife stay home. She did and bore him seven children, all of whom she trained on multiple instruments. When the family faced financial hardship during the Depression, however, Placide "allowed" his wife to resume her career.

Valaida Snow was a jazz trumpeter in the 1920s and '30s. Her mother had taught her cello, bass, violin, banjo, mandolin, harp, accordion, clarinet, saxophone, and trumpet. At fifteen, she was developing as a professional singer and trumpet player. Her talented hot jazz trumpet style, so much like that of Louis Armstrong, earned her the nickname "Little Louis." Armstrong himself called her the world's second best jazz trumpet player.

She played trumpet with greats such as Count Basie and acted on Broadway with other greats such as Ethel Waters in "Rhapsody in Black" in New York. She also performed in Europe and Asia and was a savvy businesswoman who spoke seven languages. She too could have been one of the great trumpet players, but her trumpeting career bowed to a singing and acting career that blossomed albeit it trumped her trumpeting talents.

Orchestra jobs for female trumpeters were scarce as well. The few women orchestras were beginning to hire were string players. Women addressed this employment exclusion by forming female orchestras. Expert trumpet player Mable Swint Ewer of Boston organized one of the first female orchestras in the United States in 1921. But even Ewer, when she began her early musical education at the New England conservatory, needed permission from her father before she could become a female trumpet player.

Clora Bryant's love for the trumpet began as a teen in 1941, when her brother was drafted into the army and left behind his trumpet, she picked up. Job opportunities for women did increase during the war years, but the female musicians were demeaningly called "Swing Shift Masies," a slang term indicating they were "substitutes" for the "real" male musicians who were away at war. Still, Bryant's career path began to break into the male-dominated brass bastion. She was the first woman to play publicly with Charlie Parker. She recorded with Dizzy Gillespie and played with other greats, including Louis Armstrong, Carl Perkins, and Dexter Gordon. In the 1940s she toured with the all-female Black Queens of Swing and with Billie Holiday. Her album *Gal with a Horn* was released in 1957, and later she performed jazz in the Soviet Union upon invitation by Mikhail Gorbachev.

In 1964, Marie Speziale was the first female trumpet player hired in a major orchestra (Cincinnati Symphony). And in 1973, Susan Slaughter became the first female principal trumpet to be hired by a major orchestra (St. Louis Symphony)—318 years after Johanna had trumpeted for Leopold in 1655.

Sources:
Sherrie Tucker, *Swing Shift: All-Girl Bands of the 1940s*.
http://www.susanfleet.com;
http://debbiesmusicblog.blogspot.com/2008/01/where-are-female-trumpet-players.html
http://www.msmagazine.com/winter2004/jazz.asp.
https://en.wikipedia.org/wiki/Valaida_Snow.
https://en.wikipedia.org/wiki/Clora_Bryant.
http://music.rice.edu/facultybios/speziale.shtml.
July 2010

Chapter Forty-Five
Moroccan Women

~

*W*omen in Morocco live in a country that is 99 percent Muslim, and women in the United States live in a country that is 0.8 percent Muslim. Still, women in government in both these countries do not navigate as freely as did the merchant ships of colonial days under the oldest, unbroken peace treaty in U.S history between their two countries.

The 1786 Moroccan-American Treaty of Friendship signed by Thomas Jefferson, John Adams, and the Sultan Mohammed III who declared that merchant ships sailing the Atlantic Ocean from the new US nation would be under the protection of the sultanate from Barbary pirates and could enjoy safe passage. Women's passage into politics in both these countries occurred centuries later.

The earliest Moroccan women's political organizations did not take shape until 1944, with the Women's Section of the Istiqlal Party and the Union of Moroccan Women, and in 1946, with the Akhawat al-Safaa. Two women of note in the 1940s were Malika al-Fassi, the only woman to sign the Manifesto of Independence, and Lalla Radia Ouzzani Chafdi, who helped educate, fund, and build a Fez-based high school for poor women, albeit she herself was illiterate.

Between1956 and 1970, a state feminism emerged, creating a "friendly" relationship between the state and women concerning women's rights to education, political participation, and work. Mohamed V established a commission of male Ulamas headed by Allal al-Fassi to codify the personal status code that was "outrageously disadvantageous to women, particularly in matters relating to marriage, divorce and inheritance."

In the 1980s, women's voices appeared in two women's movements. One promoted social equity through party politics, and another pointed out the gender issue and the singularity of women's demands. Out of these emerged pioneering women's associations, such as L'Association Marocaine des Femmes Democrats, L'Action Feminine, and Jossour. In 1983, the first feminist journals came out seriously addressing gender issues.

These not-for-profits of the 1980s actually began to take shape in the 1970s. Similarly, in the United States, women's studies first appeared as college courses, and the groundbreaking Title IX was passed in 1972. But not so similarly, in that the genesis for US women's organizations began not a decade, but a century earlier, specifically with the organization of the American Association of University Women (AAUW), which began in Boston in 1881 with seventeen women and now asserts a nationwide membership of one hundred thousand.

Since the 1990s, Morocco has seen a dramatic increase in women's civil-societal activism directed toward legal and protective rights, combating illiteracy (particularly in rural areas), and promoting awareness of women's issues. One million signatures collected by L'Action Feminine resulted in the 1992 amendment of the Family Code by King Hassan II. The European Commission, World Bank, and UNESCO have funded numerous seminars and workshops on issues like domestic violence, fund-raising, illiteracy, and information technology to empower women.

Also in 1992, two women were elected as members of the Parliament of Morocco. In 1997, in a thirty-member cabinet, four women were designated secretaries of states by the late Hassan II. In 2000, the first woman minister was designated to be responsible for Women's Issues, Childhood, and the Handicapped. Also that year, an unprecedented three women received ambassador assignments.

September 2002 saw three women named to government posts of Family, Immigration, Illiteracy and Non-Formal Education. That October, a gender quota system in parliamentary elections was implemented. Accordingly, thirty women were elected in the legislatures, and five more were directly elected. And in 2003, 6,024 women announced their candidacies in municipal elections. Though 127 were elected, out of a total of 22,816 positions, women constituted a mere 0.55 percent. The 2007 parliamentary elections conformed to the quota system of thirty seats for women. Four more women were directly elected, and seven women were appointed ministers.

On October 19, 2008, the monarch called on both the government and parliament to constructively cooperate. They were to put forward sensible mechanisms to ensure that a larger number of women would stand as candidates and be elected to local councils. The principal purpose, the king remarked, "is to make sure women are fairly represented in local governments, and to enable local councils to benefit from the contributions of competent Moroccan women known for their integrity, pragmatism, and concern for social well-being."

That year on October 28, Moroccan women MPs called for the elaboration of a bill to strengthen women's political participation and safeguard the right to equality, "proposing" that the bill should amend the electoral code so that women constitute one-third of seats in the 2009 municipal elections.

As it was in colonial days, friendship between these two countries was similar in 2001. Morocco was among the first Arab and Islamic states to denounce the 9/11 terrorist attacks and to declare solidarity with the American people in fighting terrorism.

And as it was in colonial days for women in government in these two countries, so it is similar for women in both these countries in 2001, as well. The 111th US Congress politically navigates with 17 percent American women and the Parliament of Morocco, after the 2007 elections, politically navigates with 10 percent Moroccan women.

Sources:

Fatima Sadiqu, University of Fez, *Women & Politics in Morocco.*
http://chartsbin.com/view/r80; http://www.state.gov/r/pa/ei/bgn/5431.
    htm.

http://www.authorstream.com/Presentation/s.mohamed-141642-
   women-politics-morocco-civil-society-family-code-education-ppt-
   powerpoint/.
September 2010

Chapter Forty-Six
Not So Bad / No Qué Lástima
~

*T*he life of Frida Kahlo began a one-hour streetcar ride away from Mexico City in the pueblo of Coyoán. In a one-story blue stucco house, La Casa Azul, shadowed by taller-than-one-story trees, Frida was born on the morning of July 6, 1907.

Her mother, a devout Catholic, was part Indian. Her father was an atheist Austro-Hungarian Jew who had emigrated from Germany at age nineteen. It was her maternal grandmother and Indian grandfather who infused her with the Mexican ancestry she celebrated her entire life.

When six, Frida was bedridden with polio for nearly a year. The disease left her with one leg shorter than the other, a deformity of which she was always self-conscious. At fifteen, she qualified for the Escuéla Nacional Preparatoria in the old Colegio de San Lldefonso in Mexico City, where women had only recently been admitted. Kahlo was one of a mere thirty-five females in a class of two thousand. She studied art, literature, law, and medicine.

It was here she first experienced the driving cultural forces that prepared her for her future in modern Mexico and the world. It was here she designed her sights on medial school at a time when women doctors were rare. It was here she began adorning her notebooks with sketches. It was here she met and set her desires on Diego Rivera, the grand muralist of Mexico whom one day she would marry, divorce, and marry again. It was here as a teen that she told her friends she wanted to have Rivera's child.

It was here at age eighteen, when the bus on which she was riding turned in front of an oncoming streetcar that impinged itself into the bus. A metal handrail literally impaled Kahlo, entering through her left hip and exiting through her genitals. A man at the scene dressed in overalls said the rod had to be removed. Without pause for thought, he pulled the metal rod out of Kahlo's body to the horrific sound of breaking bones.

Kahlo always maintained that this intrusion into her pelvis caused her inability to bear children. Though never medically validated, Kahlo believed it and endured it in a culture where motherhood defined womanhood.

In fact, she was lucky to be alive. She had incurred numerous breaks in her pelvic bone, spinal column, and collarbone. Several ribs were cracked, her right leg was broken in eleven places, and her right foot was crushed. Despite thirty-nine subsequent operations, Kahlo would be a semi-invalid the rest of her life.

Confined to bed in immobilizing splints designed to protect her many fractures, she spent a month hospitalized and the next two years in body-restrictive recovery. She did not return to her medical studies. But bedridden, she began to paint.

Though Kahlo did not become the female physician she had set out to be, her studies of science, particularly physiology, played an important role in her paintings. The glands, hearts, and other inner body organs she often included in her paintings were incredibly accurate. In *The Two Fridas*, she painted her condition anatomically correct and portrayed her condition of aloneness by being alone together with herself, the same a being alone.

Kahlo's activism in politics is portrayed in two political paintings—*My Dress Hangs There*, where aloneness also manifests itself in her depiction of one dress devoid of other dresses or any other articles of clothing, and *Marxism Will Give Health to the Sick*, where again, she is alone.

Kahlo celebrated the culture of Mexico through her ethnic style of dress and in her paintings. Yet she recognized it as a culture that restricted and defined not only her art but also her life. In *Self-Portrait on the Border Line Between Mexico and the United States*, where again she is alone, Kahlo conveyed her strong political and personal anxiety for the two countries of which she was a product.

Kahlo was part of the generation that introduced a significant female presence into the visual arts. Nonetheless, women artists in Mexico were virtually excluded from the mural movement in Mexico that was more highly valued than easel painting. Kahlo was a victim of how gender curtailed opportunities for female artists.

But when she began dating Rivera, Kahlo painted with a new confidence. She assumed his way of painting and painted what he liked. She measured her success through his affirmation. Her paintings took on value for her only when they were valued by a man. This female need to be validated by males was not unique to Kahlo at that time. It was, some say is, accepted and expected, normal behavior by women in general.

At age twenty-two, Kahlo became Diego's wife. She painted little during their early months of marriage, when she subordinated her life to his. She catered both to his needs and her need to be a good wife to him. He became her identity. Diego put her first in his life also, but somewhere after his paintings. Life together was stormy at best.

As a female painter, Kahlo received little if any encouragement from others. She painted only 143 known paintings, 55 of which are self-portraits, 8 of which show her with tears painted on her face in a surrealist style rather than anatomically correct. Thus, these 8 paintings are deeply, deeply provoking, given her anatomical knowledge. She masked her inner feelings while she unmasked them.

When asked why she painted many self-portraits, Kahlo frequently replied "porque estoy muy sola" (because I am all alone). She didn't fit anywhere in the accepted gender codes of society, as well as within herself, for she herself was part of that society. Albeit she had little respect for limitations, she herself had limits.

Perhaps if someone would have said, "You're not so bad," she would have known, shown, accepted, and celebrated the woman she was before she died in 1954.

Sources:
Martha Zamora, *Frida Kahlo*, Sarah M. Lowe; *Frida Kahlo: The Brush of Anguish*.
December 2010

Chapter Forty-Seven
Born in the USA
~

*Y*oshiko Uchida (1921–92) was born in California, pledged allegiance to the flag each morning in school, and loved her country. But her face, her eyes, her name, her heritage, and her emigrated parents indicated to others she was not an American, which she was.

Her name troubled teachers, to pronounce, and necessary questions troubled her: "Can we swim in your pool? We're Japanese." "Will the neighbors object if we move in next door?" "Do you cut Japanese hair?" And she hated it when people would compliment her on her perfect use of the English language.

She and her sister Keiko refused to attend the Japanese Language School, albeit they honored their mother by letting her teach the language to them personally. And while Yoshiko learned much Japanese culture through osmosis, she always preferred her white baby dolls, who didn't really look like her, because she always thought of herself as an American, which she was.

Yoshiko and Keiko grew up in a bungalow with a sandbox and two swings in their large backyard. with fruit trees, from which her mother made jam. Her father took the ferry to work each day. She and her sister put on shows for the neighborhood kids, roller-skated down the block, and played cops and robbers. She always thought of herself as an American, which she was.

She hated when visitors from Japan would come visit, which was often. She was embarrassed when Japanese students studying in the United States would be invited for dinner, which also was often.

When Yoshiko was in seventh grade, her junior high school was damaged by the 1933 Long Beach earthquake and condemned unsafe. She was sent to Willard Junior High on Telegraph Avenue in a white, affluent area, six blocks east of her home. Japanese American college students worked in these homes, but none lived in them, per an unwritten realtor practice. Yoshiko already knew what it was to feel unwanted in certain shops or restaurants or hotels, to be treated as if she weren't there, but being ignored everyday by classmates really scared her.

When Yoshiko was twelve, she sailed on the *Chichibu Maru* with her parents and sister to visit Japan and family there. On the ship, they dined with the deans of women at both Mills College and the University of California in Berkley, who each invited the girls to attend their universities.

During her visit in Japan, she blended in and looked like everyone else, although she longed for hot dogs, chocolate, and bathrooms with plumbing. She missed her English language, especially when asked by an old woman to read a bus sign for her and she could not. In a country where she appeared to belong, she most poignantly experienced being a foreigner, which she was.

High school years for Yoshiko were socially strained, but she excelled in her studies. She took extra classes and graduated early, and at sixteen, she enrolled at the University of California, Berkeley. Japanese American college students were excluded from the white sororities and fraternities but welcomed into the new Nisei community of student clubs for both Japanese men and women. In these student clubs, Yoshiko was finally able to socialize, date, and have fun.

She was a senior when the Japanese attacked Pearl Harbor. From that moment, all Japanese and all Japanese Americans had become the enemy. Her mother and father were not citizens because US law prevented Asians from becoming naturalized citizens. Yoshiko and Keiko were not treated as citizens, which they were.

Racist groups called for a forced eviction of all Americans of Japanese ancestry, a hatred not new. Laws restricting Japanese immigration and land ownership had existed for more than a hundred years. It was now 1942, and Congressman John Rankin had shouted on the floor of the

House, "I say it is of vital importance that we get rid of every Japanese … Damn them! Let us get rid of them now!" No such anger or action was directed toward German or Italian American immigrants or citizens whose countries were also at war with the United States.

Ten weeks later, President Franklin Roosevelt signed Executive Order 9066, authorizing the exclusion of all persons of Japanese descent. Her father was taken away for questioning. A guard remained in her home, which had been searched. All leaders of the Japanese American community, businessmen, teachers, bankers, farmers, fishermen, were apprehended and sent to prisoner-of-war camps. All were registered, numbered, tagged, and kept under armed guard.

Many were herded into buses or trains surrounded by American soldiers carrying rifles with fixed bayonets; some were forced to board militarized freighters and made to strip naked. Yoshiko, her sister, and mother were taken to live in horse stalls that reeked of urine and horse manure. She later wrote of how, in the mess hall, "A cook reached in a dishpan full of canned sausages and dropped two onto my plate with his fingers … we tried to eat but the food would not go down … we were constantly hungry."

All mail was censored. There was a morning and at 6:00 p.m. daily head count. The encampment was unconstitutional but Japanese respect for authority did not harbor thoughts of resistance or confrontation. Civil rights demonstrations and marches of the sixties had not yet been born in the USA.

The Quakers were instrumental in helping encamped students be allowed to return to school. In 1943, Yoshiko was accepted to graduate school at Smith College and was allowed to leave. But she could not leave behind the pain of those years. After graduating, she taught in a Quaker school and then sought employment that would allow more time for writing. And write she did.

Yoshiko Uchida authored almost forty works of fiction and nonfiction, all of which embodied cultural differences, ethnicity, citizenship, identity, and the racism endured by children making their way in a world of differing cultures, cultures often in conflict. A Ford Foundation Fellowship sent her to Japan for two years where she learned to appreciate the culture of her own ancestry, which she'd "hated" as a child growing up in California.

Yoshiko was a pioneer who created a body of Japanese American literature that had not previously existed, especially in children's books. Of her books, she said, "I try to stress the positive aspects of life that I want children to value and cherish. I hope they can be caring human beings who don't think in terms of labels—foreigners or Asians or whatever—but think of people as human beings. If that comes across, then I've accomplished my purpose."

Yoshiko Uchida passed away in 1992 after a prolific career, during which she wrote about being what she came to understand as an American of two cultures and what that meant when one looked as if one was not born in the USA, which she was.

Sources:

Yoshiko Uchida, *The Invisible Thread.*

http://en.wikipedia.org/wiki/Yoshiko_Uchida.

July 2012

Chapter Forty-Eight
Rosie the Radical
~

S he left high school to care for her mother but returned as a woman to graduate in 1934. As a 1940s' social activist, she joined the NAACP. She was secretary of her branch from 1943 to 1956. She trained youths to protest the segregated public library and worked for the release of the nine young Scottsboro Boys, who had been accused of rape, quickly tried by an all-white jury, and sentenced to death by a lower court in Alabama. The Supreme Court ordered a new trial for the Scottsboro Boys. The case is now widely considered a miscarriage of justice, particularly highlighted the use of all-white juries.

She worked in Montgomery Voters League voter registration drives when registering was difficult, elusive, and often dangerous for black citizens. Failed twice by the registrar, her own voting right was not recognized until her third brave attempt. She achieved this right few blacks were able to secure. She attended multiple classes and seminars concerned with civil rights reform, most notably a workshop at a training ground for labor organizers and social activists in the summer of 1955. There, she began to appreciate and understand leadership skills necessary to be effective when organizing for social causes. That winter, on December 1, she boarded a bus.

As a thirty-year social activist, she did not plan to personally stand up for justice that day. However, when asked to move so that a white could have her seat in the first row of the black section, she defied the local segregation ordinance and remained seated. Racial abuse on buses was common. Refusal to move was dangerous. Blacks had been arrested, beaten, even killed for disobeying bus drivers. On December 1, 1955, Montgomery police also boarded a bus and arrested Rosa Parks.

That night, Alabama State University professor Jo Ann Robinson of the Women's Political Caucus, inspired by Parks's courage, printed 52,000 flyers urging a bus boycott. Doctors, lawyers, professors, and white-collar workers joined domestic workers and blue-collar laborers and shut down the public transit system. People walked from everywhere to everywhere. Six months later, an Alabama federal court declared segregated bus service unconstitutional. The ruling was appealed but upheld in the US Supreme Court. On December 20, 1956, the boycott ended after 381 days and ended segregated seating on Montgomery, Alabama's busses.

Of Parks's refusal to move, it has been written that she was tired of her day's work as a seamstress. She said, she was "tired of giving in." She recalled in a speech how history has recorded "that my feet were hurting ... but the real reason was ... I felt that I had a right to be treated as any other passenger. We [blacks] had endured that kind of treatment for too long." In 1963 at the March on Washington, Parks commented, "The only thing that bothered me was that we waited so long to make this protest." Seems she was more than a seamstress.

Still, one year and sixteen days previous to the Supreme Court decision, on December 1, 1955, the night of Rosa Parks' arrest, black women in the Montgomery Improvement Association looked on as it named as its president Martin Luther King, Jr., who ultimately gained torch-bearing fame through ardent speeches as he spoke the fundamental/radical voice given to the civil rights movement by trailblazer Rosa Louise McCauley Parks (Rosie the Radical).

Source:

Darlene Clark Hine, *Black Women in America*.

http://www.achievement.org/autodoc/page/par0pro-1.

December 2005

Chapter Forty-Nine
Cherokee Ms. Chief
~

Her great-grandfather was one of the Native American Indians who was displaced in the removal order signed by President Andrew Jackson in the 1830s. He was among those brutally forced to walk more than 1.200 miles from their homes in the Southeast to newly designated "Indian territory" in Oklahoma—an inhumane journey that would come to be known as the Trail of Tears. At the time, a significant number of people in America still questioned whether Native American Indians were human or even had souls. In the 1787 US Constitution determining representation, Native American Indians were not counted as a person. (See Article I, Section 2.)

Her father was a full-blooded Cherokee. Her mother, who acculturated to Cherokee life, was Dutch/Irish. They lived on a 160-acre tract of land that had been given to her grandfather as part of a settlement the federal government made for forcing the Cherokee to relocate to Oklahoma.

Wilma Pearl Mankiller, born in 1945, was the sixth of eleven children and spent her early childhood on this tract of land. The family was destitute. Ms. Mankiller recalled she never really felt poor growing up, albeit her home had no electricity, indoor plumbing, or telephones.

During World War II, the United States Army exercised eminent domain for military purposes to expand Camp Gruber and now took the Oklahoma land of forty-five Cherokee families, including the Mankillers. Her father thought he could make a better life in California and, in 1956, agreed to relocate under the Bureau of Indian Affairs' Indian Relocation Program. This program to relocate Native American Indians was conceptualized by the official, now head of the BIA, who had devised the program that had interned the Japanese during World War II. The pattern in both broke up communities and families.

However, Wilma's family's life in San Francisco did not improve. Promises made to the family were not kept, money did not arrive, and jobs were few. Her father became a warehouse worker and a union organizer. The children were homesick, and the family remained poor.

In an interview with *The New York Times* in 1993, Ms. Mankiller described the move as "my own little Trail of Tears … the United States government, through the BIA, was again trying to settle the 'Indian problem' by removal. I learned through this ordeal about the fear and anguish that occur when you give up your home, your community, and everything you have ever known to move far away to a strange place. I cried for days, not unlike the children who had stumbled down the Trail of Tears so many years before. I wept tears … tears from my history, from my tribe's past. They were Cherokee tears."

At age seventeen, Mankiller married and moved to Oakland, California where she birthed two daughters and returned to school. She took night courses at Skyline Jr. College and then at San Francisco State University while she worked for the Oakland public schools as a coordinator of Indian programs. While in the bay area, she witnessed the 1969 Occupation of Alcatraz by Native American people of varying tribes.

The occupation's intent was to call attention to governmental injustices toward Native American people and, specifically, to regain Indian sovereignty over the island in order to build a center for Native American studies. The center was to include an American Indian spiritual center, an ecology center, and an American Indian museum. The occupiers cited treatment under the relocation policies and accused the US government of breaking numerous Indian treaties. It has been recorded that the United States broke all treaties with the Native American Indians. The occupation changed Mankiller's life. She became aware that the world needed to become aware of the plight of Native American Indian people who, had rights too.

The Trail of Broken Treaties, a cross-country protest from the West Coast to Washington, DC, in autumn 1972, was designed to bring attention to Native American Indian issues, such as treaty rights, living standards, and inadequate housing. A position paper was drawn up to reestablish the sovereignty of the Indian nations.

Mankiller divorced in 1974 and, three years later, returned with her daughters to live on her grandfather's land in Oklahoma in a quest to help her own people. She took an entry-level job with the Cherokee Nation and volunteered in tribal affairs and for campaigns seeking new health and school programs. She earned a bachelor's degree in the social sciences from Flaming Rainbow University and took graduate courses in community planning through the University of Arkansas. She became an economic stimulus coordinator for the Cherokee Nation and focused on community self-help. When she got this position, there were no female executives, and she had no agenda to become chief.

In 1981, she founded and was director of the community development department of the Cherokee Nation that helped develop rural water systems and rehabilitate housing. She began to develop programs on the philosophy that Native Americans could solve their own problems. Her programs increased revenue for the tribe and called attention to her and to her work. The tribe's principal chief, Ross Swimmer, selected her as his running mate in his 1983 reelection campaign.

While campaigning, she received criticism—not for her political views but because she was a woman. She recalled it was the most hurtful experience she had ever been through—that some people felt the Cherokee would be the laughing stock of the all the tribes if they had a woman who was in the second highest position in the tribe. That said, she said, "I thought that the idea that gender had anything to do with leadership, or that leadership had anything to do with gender was foolish, and I could see no point in even beginning to try to debate that non-issue with anybody, so I just continued on." And continue on she did.

Victory made her the first woman to become deputy chief of the Cherokee Nation. When Swimmer resigned two years later to become assistant secretary for Indian Affairs at the Department of the Interior, Mankiller succeeded him as principal chief, won office in her own right in 1987, and was reelected with 83 percent of the vote in 1991. During her three terms, Mankiller reinvigorated the Cherokee Nation through community-development projects, in which men and women worked collectively for the common good.

As the tribe's leader, she was both the principal guardian of centuries of Cherokee tradition and customs, including legal codes, and chief executive of a tribe with an annual budget of $150 million. One of her priorities was to direct much of this income back into new or expanded health care, job training, and educational programs. She oversaw the construction of new schools, centers for job training, and health clinics.

Her administration founded the Cherokee Nation Community Development Department, revived the tribal Sequoyah High School in Tahlequah, and saw a population increase of Cherokee Nation citizens from 55,000 to 156,000. "Prior to my election," said Mankiller, "young Cherokee girls would never have thought that they might grow up and become chief."

Mankiller left office in 1995 due to health concerns but remained a force in tribal affairs and took a position as guest professor at Dartmouth College. She won several prestigious awards; was honored in the Oklahoma Women's Hall of Fame and inducted into the National Women's Hall of Fame; and was awarded the Presidential Medal of Freedom, the nation's highest civilian honor.

Twenty years after the Occupation of Alcatraz, legislation was passed in 1989 to allow for a Native American museum to be built on the Mall in Washington, DC, where the National Museum of the American Indian (NMAI), a Smithsonian Institution, opened in 2004. The trail of Wilma Pearl Mankiller, a very humane journey, ended in April 2010.

Sources:

http://gos.sbc.edu/m/mankiller.html

http://en.wikipedia.org/wiki/Wilma_Mankiller.

August 2012

Chapter Fifty
Puertoriqueña Doctor/Nurse

~

*D*r. Dolores Mercedes Piñero (1892–1975) was born in San Juan, Puerto Rico when the island was still a Spanish colony. Following her primary and secondary education, Piñero was sent to Boston. She became fluent in English and, in 1913, earned her medical degree from Boston's College of Physicians and Surgeons. Dr. Piñero was one of the first four Puerto Rican women to earn a medical degree. The women she followed were María Elisa Rivera Díaz, MD, and Ana Janer, MD, in 1909 and Palmira Gatell, MD, in 1910. As a new doctor, Piñero returned to Puerto Rico to set up her medical and anesthesia practice.

In 1917, with Puerto Rico a Spanish colony no longer but now a US territory, and in the advent of the United States entry into World War I, President Woodrow Wilson signed the Jones-Shafroth act, granting US citizenship to the inhabitants of Puerto Rico. US citizenship meant that Puerto Rican men were eligible for the draft and could volunteer to join the army. Few chose to volunteer. After two months, Wilson signed a compulsory military service act and 20,000 Puerto Ricans were eventually drafted to serve during World War I.

Piñero applied for a position as a military surgeon, only to be turned down because of her gender. The army believed it had enough male physicians to cover the army's needs. However, after writing a letter to the Surgeon General of the United States Army in Washington, DC, Dr. Piñero, an anesthesiologist, received a telegram ordering her to report to Camp Las Casas in Puerto Rico. There, she was assigned to the Medical Service Corps of the Army Medical Department.

The army was affected by the shortage of male physicians specializing in anesthesiology. At the time, anesthesiology was a low-salary specialty, from which male physicians refrained. Thus, it was a specialty in which female physicians were able to practice. But anesthesia is required in all operating rooms, and military operating rooms were no exception. Therefore, the army reluctantly began hiring women physicians as civilian contract employees. As civilian contract physicians, women had a negative, gender-disparate status within the military. Civilian contract physicians could not wear uniforms and had little authority, albeit they were medical doctors with gender-equal medical credentials. Still, it was an opportunity for women to serve in the war effort.

Piñero signed such a contract with the army in 1918 and was assigned to the Army General Hospital of Fort Brooke, Florida, as an anesthesiologist. She and four male colleagues received orders to open a four hundred-bed hospital to combat the swine flu epidemic that had infected one-quarter of all soldiers and killed more than 55,000 American troops. After the flu epidemic ended, Piñero was ordered back to the army base hospital at San Juan, where, after the war, she returned to her private practice. Among the nurses who served with Piñero during the war was Rosa González.

Rosa González, RN (1889–1981), was born and raised in the town of Lares, Puerto Rico, where she received her primary and secondary education. As Dr. Piñero, she was a child on the island when Spain ceded Puerto Rico to the United States in accord with the 1898 Treaty of Paris.

González earned her nursing certificate from the Presbyterian Hospital School of Nursing in San Juan in 1909. And in 1914, she went to New York City to complete her RN licensed certificate. Two years later, with her certificate in hand, González returned to her homeland. She organized a clinic in the city of Arecibo and, that same year, founded and presided over the Association of Registered Nurses of Puerto Rico. The following year, González wrote her first book, *Diccionario Médico para la Enfermera* (*Nurse's Medical Dictionary*).

During World War I, González was sent to the Puerto Rican city of Ponce to assist Dr. Dolores Piñero and four male doctors in opening the hospital to combat the spread of swine flu. After her war service, González served as the director of Puerto Rico's Presbyterian Hospital School of Nursing from 1919 to 1924.

In 1926, she started a magazine for nurses called *Puerto Rico* and she founded several institutions. Among those she organized were the Amarosa Sanitarium in the town of Villaba (1929), the school of the Institute of Medical Surgery (1930), and the nursing school on the grounds of the School of Tropical Medicine in San Juan (1931). In her hometown of Lares in 1936, González organized the first women's clinic and served as its director until 1940.

Her book *Los Hechos Desconocidos* (*Unknown Facts*) was published in 1929. She dedicated it to the governor of Puerto Rico, the Puerto Rican legislature, the medical association, the Puerto Rican Nurses Association, and the Association of Puerto Rican Women Surrogates. She used her book to promote the establishment of a Nurse Examiners Board in Puerto Rico that, in fact, was established in 1930, the year following publication of her book.

As a women's rights activist, González denounced the discriminatory practices against women in the health care professions. She believed that the "medical class" discriminated against female nurses and stated this clearly in her book where she wrote:

> In our country any man who is active in a political party, will be considered capable of handling an administrative position, regardless of how inept he is.
>
> To this day the 'Medical Class' has not accepted nurses who have the same goal as doctors: the well-being of the patient. Both professions need each other in order to be successful.

When the United States entered World War II, González was named director of the Nurses Services of the American Red Cross in Puerto Rico. Until her death of natural causes at age ninety-two, she continued to provide free medical services for the children in Guaynabo where she resided.

Sources: http://www.history.com/this-day-in-history/puerto-ricans-become-u-s-citizens-are-recruited-for-war-effort, Wikipedia specific to each woman.
November 2012

Chapter Fifty-One
Puerto Rican Flag /
Professor / Flying Nun

⁓

*L*ola Rodríguez de Tió (1843–1924) believed in women's rights, the abolition of slavery, and the independence of Puerto Rico. She is considered the first Puerto Rican poetess to receive recognition throughout all of Latin America.

Her father, of Venezuelan descent, founded the Colegio de Abogados de Puerto Rico (Puerto Rico Law School). Her mother was a descendant of the explorer and first Spanish governor of Puerto Rico, Juan Ponce de León. Rodríguez de Tió, although home-tutored, was very assertive in her early years. At seventeen, against the strict norm of the time, she broke convention, demanded she be allowed to wear her hair short, did so then, and then continued to do so throughout her life.

A political activist, writer, and book importer, Rodríguez often wrote articles against the Spanish regime that were printed in the local press, as would be tolerated by the regime. In 1867, and then again in 1889, she and her husband were banished from Puerto Rico by the Spanish-appointed governors.

On their first exile, they lived in Venezuela. And on their second, they moved to New York, where she assisted Cuban revolutionaries. Later they moved to Cuba where their home became a gathering point for politicians and intellectuals as well as exiled Puerto Ricans. They resided in Cuba until their respective deaths.

In 1868, inspired by and supporting a quest for Puerto Rico's independence, Rodríguez wrote the patriotic lyrics to the existing tune of "La Borinquena." In 1901, she founded and was an elected member of the Cuban Academy of Arts and Letters and was an inspector of the local school system. She was well known in Cuba for her patriotic poetry about both Puerto Rico and Cuba.

It is believed by some that the design and colors of the Puerto Rican Flag, adopted in 1954, came from her idea of having the same flag as Cuba with the colors reversed. Puerto Rico has honored her memory by naming schools and avenues after her. Lola Rodríguez de Tió is buried in Cuba.

Ana María O'Neill (1894–1981) was an advocate of women's rights, an educator, and an author. She received her primary and secondary education in Aguadilla, Puerto Rico, the town of her birth, and earned her teacher's certificate in 1915 from the Normal School of the University of Puerto Rico in San Juan. After teaching in Puerto Rico, she went to New York to continue her education at Columbia University, from which she earned her master's degree in education in 1927.

O'Neill returned to Puerto Rico two years later to become the first female professor in the department of commerce at the University of Puerto Rico, where she taught until 1951. As a women's rights activist, she urged women to participate in every aspect of civic life and to defend their right to vote.

She earned a diploma as a cooperative leader from the Rochdale Institute of the National School of Cooperativism. She fought for the cooperative movement in Puerto Rico and was instrumental in the passing of the legislation entitled "The General Law of Cooperative Societies." In 1946, O'Neill founded the Cooperative Institute of the University of Puerto Rico. In 1948, she authored *Etica Para la Era Atómica* (*Ethics for the Atomic Age*), which was acclaimed and recognized with a literary award from Northwestern University. In 1966, she was honored by the Union of American Women, who named her the 1966 "Woman of Puerto Rico." That same year, she was recognized by the cooperative establishment of the island and was named "Woman of the Americas." O'Neill also authored *Psicología de la Comunicación* (*The Psychology of Communication*), which was published in 1986, five years after her death.

Marie Teresa Ríos (1917–99) was born in Brooklyn, of Puerto Rican and Irish heritage. As a child, she displayed an interest in writing. As a young woman in the 1930s, she married Humbert Joseph Versace, a 1933 graduate of West Point, with whom she had five children. Their son Rocky Versace, executed by the Viet Cong in 1965, was a Medal of Honor recipient. Another son, Richard Versace, was the first person of Puerto Rican descent to coach an NBA team, the Indian Pacers from 1988 to 1990.

During World War II, Ríos drove army trucks and buses and served as a pilot for the Civil Air Patrol. She wrote and edited for publications such the *Armed Forces Stars & Stripes* and *Gannett* and for various newspapers internationally in Guam and Germany and nationally in South Dakota and Wisconsin.

Ríos taught creative writing at the University of Pittsburgh and was on the staff of Wisconsin's Rhinelander Writers Conference. She wrote under the pen name "Tere Ríos" and published her first book, *An Angel Grows Up*, in 1957. Her second book, *Brother Angel*, followed in 1963. And her third book, *The Fifteenth Pelican*, debuted in 1965. *The Fifteenth Pelican* is the book on which *The Flying Nun* television show was based. The TV series, starring Sally Field, ran from 1968 to 1970.

In 1958, Ríos was named Wisconsin Writer of the Year. Upon her death, her ashes were buried with her husband at Arlington National Cemetery.

Sources:
Wikipedia specific to each woman.
December 2012

Chapter Fifty-Two
Her Words / His Music

~

*B*efore Bob Fosse's *Chicago*, before Walt Disney's *Mary Poppins*, before Rodgers and Hammerstein's *Sound of Music*, there were Maurine Watkins, P. L. Travers, and Sr. Mary Francis Borgia, O.S.F.

During the roaring twenties, Maureen Watkins, a savvy but novice *Chicago Tribune* newspaper reporter, was assigned to cover police reports from a "feminine" perspective. Watkins, an educated journalist, had studied at Butler University, at Radcliffe in their PhD program, and at Yale School of Drama under the renowned teacher of American playwrights George Pierce Baker. Baker awarded his highest grade ever to Watkins, whose classmates included Eugene O'Neill and Philip Barry.

On March 12, 1924, Watkins was assigned to cover the crime of a cabaret singer with a long history of affairs, who allegedly had shot her current lover. Knowing her crime report would be relegated to the back pages, Watkins spiced it up with wry humor. Less than a month later, another married woman killed her lover. She put on a record before phoning her husband to tell him she had shot an intruder who tried to make love to her and that she shot him to save her honor. Watkins's headline on this crime read "Woman Plays Jazz as Victim Dies."

Watkins didn't get a byline until her third article on these jealous female killers of men who "done them wrong" when another woman, an illiterate immigrant, was sentenced to life in prison. Watkins' stories now made the front page with readers following "Murderess Row."

With the women's trials resolved and yesterday's news, Watkins was reassigned, lost interest, left the *Tribune*, relocated to New York, and returned to Yale to rewrite her articles into a stage comedy she titled

Chicago. It opened December 30, 1926, on Broadway, was a smash hit, and opened in Chicago in September 1927. Watkins was famous.

Plans for a musical version in the 1950s were stifled because Watkins vehemently refused to the sell the rights. She became a recluse and faded into obscurity. It was not until after her death in 1969 (when she was so forgotten the *New York Times* did not even print an obituary), that Bob Fosse finally obtained the rights and reinvented *Chicago* into a 1975 musical with all his jazz.

The first *Mary Poppins* book (there were four) was written by P. L. Travers in 1934. Ten years later, on a night before Christmas at bedtime, Walt Disney fortuitously heard his eleven-year-old daughter laughing out loud and stepped into her room to learn why. It was because of the *Mary Poppins* book she was reading, a book she and her mom petitioned Walt to make into a movie.

The following year, Pamela Travers was in New York, and Walt sent his brother Roy to meet with her about a possible movie. Roy was unable to convince Travers to sign over the rights. But Walt was persistent. He was very successful, and he continually sought new stories with which to work his Disney magic. He repeatedly attempted to secure the rights, and Travers repeatedly refused—for more than twenty years.

Basically, Travers wanted to preserve the character of the nanny she had created in her book, and Disney wanted to create a nanny to entertain his audiences. Walt was hard to resist, and he did persist. In 1959, he sent two representatives to London with a new offer for Travers. Though Pamela stood firm, she was advised to be practical and accept. At a time when her book sales were paltry, selling the rights would mean an income for life that could be substantial. She agreed, retaining copyrights to any material she wrote but gave up full rights to the stories. The stories were now Walt's to magically interpret.

Travers's *Mary Poppins* became Disney's *Mary Poppins*. Travers became a consultant, offering conscientious consultation, much of which Disney considered but skirted. In the end, her name appeared in small type at the beginning opening credits. Realistically, no one knew or cared how *Mary Poppins* had come to be.

At the movie premiere in 1964, Pamela cried as her *Mary Poppins* appeared before her so shockingly his. And while she telegraphed Disney of his splendid film, she maintained that the real *Mary Poppins* remained within the covers of her books.

Chicago-born Walt Disney died of lung cancer on December 15, 1966. Pamela Travers lived mostly as a recluse in London until her death in 1995, when Disney ads in trade magazines showed Mickey Mouse in tears.

The hills were not yet alive with the sound of music when the curtains opened. It was just a high school play with music about a postulant named Maria. *One Family Sings*, based on the 1949 book *The Trapp Family Singers* by Maria von Trapp, was adapted for the stage by Sr. M. Francis Borgia, O.S.F. and premiered as the 1953 senior class play at Alvernia High School in Chicago.

The first thoughts of producing this play with music were voiced in December 1952 during a lunch discussion brainstorming for a suitable play for that school year. It was mentioned it would be good to see a group work out the story of the *Trapp Family Singers*. It was a family story, and the soul of the family was a woman. It was a perfect fit for this all-girls Catholic high school that always maintained a rich choral group and, that year, had a very gifted choral director.

Gradually the discussions moved from the cons of such an undertaking to the pros. Rights to adapt the book would be needed, and the baroness was contacted. Her authorization came by telegram: "Permission granted if play strictly follows book." (Signed) Mrs. Maria Augusta Trapp. And so the stage script was written.

The school learned that the Trapp family (living in Vermont since the early 1940s) would be traveling through Chicago on a concert tour and invited them to a performance. They accepted. During intermission, the baroness took the mike and spoke with enthusiasm about the performance. As a grand finale, the family and the parallel student cast sang the closing number for an endlessly applauding audience. The impact of seeing her story on stage perhaps emboldened consideration toward future productions.

Three years later, Wolfgang Reinhardt (son of the famous stage director Max Reinhardt) offered the baroness ten thousand dollars to make a film. Maria signed, inadvertently giving away all her rights, including royalties. Wolfgang later offered nine thousand dollars in immediate cash. Maria, in need of money, accepted. *Die Trapp Familie* (1956) and *Die Trapp Familie in Amerika* (1958) found success in Germany, much of Europe, and South America.

In North America, Mary Martin and husband/manager Richard Halliday were looking for a project. They were shown the German films and really liked the story but met resistance securing the rights. Their friend, Broadway producer Leland Hayward, agreed to coproduce a Broadway show and, thus, was able to obtain the rights. Though not obliged, Hayward paid the baroness three-eighths of 1 percent royalties from the Broadway show, for which she was grateful.

Richard Rogers and Oscar Hammerstein II were asked to write a song for the play. They preferred to write a score. The play opened in 1959 to poor reviews and then ran for 1,443 performances, closing in 1963 with plans for a movie. But before the movie could be filmed, all rights needed to be in hand.

Back in 1955, Row, Peterson, and Co. had obtained permission to publish *One Family Sings* as a play that could be performed by other schools. Thus, rights to Sr. M. Francis Borgia's play had to be rescinded before the movie could be undertaken. Once accomplished, the movie version opened in 1965, and sounds of one family singing in her high school halls long ago gave way forever to the hills now alive with the sound of his music.

Sources:

Chicago, Maurine Watkins, Thomas H. Pauly, Ed.

Valerie Lawson, *Mary Poppins, She Wrote*

One Family Sings: A Full-Length Play in two acts: Adapted by Sister M. Francis Borgia, O.S.F, 1955

http://www.archives.gov/publications/prologue/2005/winter/vontrapps.html

My personal correspondence with former Sister M. Francis Borgia, in her now public position as founder and president of New Momentum for Human Unity.

October 2012

Conclusion

~

So, as I review the words I have positioned in this book for you to read—words about the diverse and accomplished women revealed in my research, I ponder why these words and why these women? And once again, as in *Cherry Blossoms*, the answer is the same. Because!

Because when we do not acknowledge the myriad of historic contributions by women of countless colors and cultures and do not know the women themselves, we are cheated—cheated of the countless historic strengths that connect us globally as women. Without knowing our strong history and its strong women, women tend to be and tend to be perceived as weak, when in fact women are strong, dam water strong, in the halls, in the hills - in all women globally.

Because with the strength of your/women's history, you can be emboldened to continue or even to begin to take steps to do the great things already in your head and heart, and see the impact that will have on you as well as on women, children and men, in your personal circles and publicly in a world that circles the globe.

Because when we do not know where women have gone and what women have done, we often question if we can go and if we can do. The empowerment that comes from knowing your/women's history embodies you, and enables you to know you can.

Thus, I dare to avow that, reading this book that celebrates women who, without support or encouragement to achieve, did achieve—women who braved scathing, ubiquitous disadvantages—has brought about a change in you, a change that will now advantage and strengthen you equal to the strong (but once virtually unknown) historic women in this book.

Make your own women's history in whatever manner you chose. Build your own dam of water! Score your own words for music! Hear their sounds roar and soar, that other women may chose to roar and soar as you.

Thank you for taking the time to read your history.

Respectfully,
bjz
countherhistory.wordpress.com

Thanks to Women

Black FLOTUS

Children's Magazine

Chocolate Chip Cookies

Circular Saw

Civil Rights

Cloud Composition

Computer Software

Dam Technology

Dishwasher

Drumming Communication

Essence Magazine

Flood Prevention Technology

Harpers' Bazaar

Her Midnight Ride

Hurricane Tower Structure

Investigative Reporting

Japanese American Literature

Kabuki

Kevlar

Ladies' Home Journal

Latina magazine

Lear's magazine

Margarita Cocktail

Mary Poppins

Midwifery

Mother's Day

Ms. magazine

NAACP

Natural Births

Peace Possibilities

Puerto Rican Flag

Quilts

Safe Abortions

Soulard Market

The Flying Nun

The First Trapp Family musical

Underground RR

Washing Machine

Weather Satellite

Women's Shelters

XX/XY sex identified

Velma & Roxie

Recommended Reading

〜

A Vindication of the Rights of Whores
      Gail Pheterson
An Imperfect God: George Washington, His Slaves, and the Creation of America
      Henry Wiencek
And If I Perish
      Evelyn M. Monahan and Rosemary Neidel-Greenlee
Anne Morrow Lindbergh: First Lady of the Air
      Kathleen C. Winters
Black and White Sat Down Together: The Reminiscences of an NAACP Founder
      Ralph Luker
Black Women in America [Business and Professions]
      Darlene Clark Hine
Chicago
      Maurine Watkins, Thomas H. Pauly, Ed.
Cleopatra
      Ed. Don Nardo
Constitutional Law and Politics
      David M. O'Brien
Eye on the Struggle: Ethel Payne the First Lady of the Black Press
      James McGrath Morris
Freedom's Daughters: The Unsung Heroines of the Civil Rights Movement from 1830 to 1970
      Lynne Olson

Frida Kahlo
    Sarah M. Lowe
Frida Kahlo: The Brush of Anguish
    Martha Zamora
Gee's Bend Quilts, and Beyond
    Mary Lee Bendolph
Gender, desire, and sexuality in T.S. Eliot
    Cassandra Laity, Nancy K. Gish
Girls Think of Everything
    Catherine Thimmesh
Goddesses, Whores, Wives, and Slaves
    Sarah B. Pomeroy
Grace & Glory: A Century of Women in the Olympics
    Jan Leder
Harem Years: The Memoirs of an Egyptian Feminist (1879-1924)
    Huda Shaarawi
Mary Poppins, She Wrote
    Valerie Lawson
Mothers and Daughters of Invention
    Autumn Stanley
Nike is a Goddess: The History of Women in Sports
    Lissa Smith, ed.
One Family Sings: A Full-Length Play in two acts:
    Adapted by Sister M. Francis Borgia, O.S.F.
Patriots in Petticoats
    Patricia Edwards Clyne
Swing Shift: All-Girl Bands of the 1940s
    Sherrie Tucker
The Invisible Thread
    Yoshiko Uchida
The Law of Sex Discrimination
    Ralph J. Lindgren & Nadine Taub
The Lively Commerce
    Charles Winick & Paul M. Kinsie

The Trapp Family Singers
  Maria von Trapp
The Women of ENIAC
  W. Barkley Fritz
Thomas Jefferson and Sally Hemings: An American Controversy
  Annette Gordon-Reed
Trespassers, Beware!: Lyda Burton Conley and the Battle for Huron Place Cemetery
  Kim Dayton
When the Drummers Were Women
  Layne Redmond
Women Composers
  Carol Plantamura
Women Making Music
  Ed. Jane Boers and Judith Tick
Women & Politics in Morocco
  Fatima Sadiqi
Working Without Uniforms
  Helen Rameriz-Odell

Appendix

~

*W*hen writing history, new facts often are discovered and need to be appended. In my first book, *From Cherry Blossoms to Cell Phones,* this occurred in Chapter Two: *One Woman/Every Baby,* about Dr. Virginia Apgar; and in Chapter Sixteen: *Business Women of Fashion* about Ellen Demorest. What I wrote and what I later learned follow:

In "One Woman / Every Baby," I highlighted Virginia Apgar, MD, (1909–74) and her establishment of the APGAR score, the medical test she developed due to her concern with the high infant mortality rate of the time. The medical research she conducted between 1949 and 1958 documented that the first twenty-four hours after birth held the highest infant mortality risk. Thus, Dr. Apgar designed a test to be administered one minute, and then again five minutes, after birth. I wrote that since the 1950s the APGAR score has been administered to every baby born in a medical facility everywhere in the world. I wrote that the APGAR score has saved countless lives, and that it is considered a standard worldwide. However, something that never surfaced in my research (and thus I did not write in my original column of October 2003), I append here.

In 2014, I attended the International Women's Day luncheon hosted by the International Trade Club of Chicago and held at Chicago's Union League Club. The keynote speaker Michéle Ledgerwood, senior associate with CSIS, the Center for Strategic and International Studies in Washington, DC, was sharing many statistical facts pertinent to women. One she shared was of the dramatic international decline in infant mortality rates since the 1950s.

Bingo! A *bright* light went off in my head! Eleven years after I had written my column in 2003, I made a connection between Dr. Apgar, the countless number of lives she saved since the 1950s, and the international decline in infant mortality rate statistics since the 1950s. This was powerful to me. But to whom else? Who else knew?

I surmised, indubitably, that I was the only woman in the room of approximately six hundred attendees celebrating IWD who not only had made that connection but also even knew the APGAR score was developed by a woman. It underscored the importance of knowing women's history; women's historic achievements; and women's impact socially, civically, globally, and personally.

After lunch, I spoke with Ms. Ledgerwood, who was *not* aware of Dr. Apgar but was enticed by the connection between Dr. Apgar and the statistical data. Subsequently, we have shared emails. In one she wrote, "I have ordered your *Thesaurus of Women* … and look forward to reading it and using it as a reference for my talks!" I was honored. Michèle is a brilliant woman!

And now, in keeping with my passion to proclaim the women's history I know to others, I am happy to tell you of the link between Dr. Virginia Apgar and the dramatic decline in infant mortality rates, globally. Two links follow for statistical fact checking:

Infant mortality rates in the United States from 1950 (20.5) to 2010 (4.0), according to year, race, and gestation period (http://www.infoplease.com/ipa/A0779935.html)

UN World Population stats – Figures are from the 2011 revision of the United Nations World Population Prospects report, by five years averages, and the CIA World Factbook (http://en.wikipedia.org/wiki/List_of_countries_by_infant_mortality_rate)

* * * * *

In "Business Women of Fashion," Ellen Demorest (1824–1898) is one of three women highlighted in brief bios on each. I wrote of how, in the mid-1800s, Demorest started a business for women who wished to appear fashionable in public but who might not have the means to employ expensive dressmakers. I wrote that Demorest had a special interest in improving the lives of women and that she employed more than two hundred diverse women in her business. She paid and treated all equally and invited any wealthy, influential customers who disapproved to shop elsewhere. I also wrote that she is credited with having developed the paper pattern and, together with her husband, mass-produced them, which allowed for reasonable pattern pricing and for dressmaking to be done at home from accurate, fashionable paper patters. Thus, their business linked fashion with the needy women she wished to serve. But the importance to women, especially women in business, of something that manifested itself later, and what I did not write in my original column of November 2005, I append here.

In 2014, I produced a power point program titled *Lady MBAs* (Masters of Business Administration) that allowed for expanded information on several businesswomen. Regarding Mme. Demorest, I included that she encouraged women to enter the business world, that she funded an early woman's college that performed social welfare work, and that she was treasurer of the New York Medical College for Women and was the chairperson of a shelter for women and children. Her patterns became ubiquitous in America, with more than three million sold in her peak business year, 1876.

But the new information I included that commands the largest "aghast" response from my audiences and what I now wish to tell you is that, in the 1880s, she and her husband's mass production of paper pattern business began to decline, in large part because the Demorests failed to patent their paper pattern idea, and the competition from others now merchandising paper patterns, in particular Ebenezer Butterick, the man often credited with having originated the idea when credit might well belong to a woman, whom you now know.

Index